Contents

INTRODUCTION   5

RECLAMATION PART 1   7
    "Home Movies" (into "Bob's Burgers")   7
    "The Oblongs"   9
    "Mission Hill"   13

RECLAMATION PART 2   15
    "Family Guy," "The Cleveland Show," and "American Dad!"   15
    "Futurama"   18
    "King of the Hill"   20
    The Animation Show (2003-8) featuring Don Hertzfeldt   22
    "The Boondocks" (into "Black Jesus" and Toonami)   24

MY ADVICE AND MY STORY. BY ANGUS OBLONG.   28

WILLIAMS STREET: RECYCLED ANIMATION   33
    "Space Ghost Coast to Coast"   34
    "The Brak Show" and Adult Swim music   36
    "Harvey Birdman, Attorney at Law"   39
    Seventy-Thirty's "Sealab 2021" (into "Frisky Dingo")   42

ANIMATION   44
    "Aqua Teen Hunger Force" et al.   44
    "Squidbillies"   48
    "12 Oz. Mouse"   50
    "The Jellies" (and "Loiter Squad")   51
    "Lucy, The Daughter of the Devil"   53
    "Metalocalypse"   54

"Mongo Wrestling Alliance" 56
"Rick and Morty" 57
"The Venture Bros." 58
"Tom Goes to the Mayor" 60

LIVE-ACTION   62

Tim Heidecker and Eric Wareheim continued 62
"Check It Out! with Dr. Steve Brule" 65
"Delocated" and "Neon Joe, Werewolf Hunter" 68
"Eagleheart" 69

STOP-MOTION   71

"Moral Orel" into "Mary Shelley's Frankenhole" 71
"Robot Chicken," Seth Green, and Stoopid Buddy Stoodios 73

LIVE STREAM ONLINE PROGRAMMING   76

BUMPS, ADS, AND PROMOS   77

RESEARCH AND THEORY: CARTOONOGRAPHY   80

GLOSSARIES.   89

Comedy 89
Animation 91
Film 93

COLOR ART   96

Illustration and photo donations courtesy of the following genuinely kind folks: Seth MacFarlane; Ralph Steadman; Linda Lautrec and Johnny Legend; Brenda Feldman, Tom Root, and Seth Green at Stoopid Buddy Stoodios; Victoria Biggers; Jennifer Lee Pryor; Chuck Jones Center for Creativity; Dave Thomas; Tim and Eric at Abso Lutely Productions; Don Hertzfeldt at Bitter Films; and Angus Oblong.

The Adult Swim course has had a lot of press over the years but special thanks to a few of the early pieces: "G4TV: Filter," 3/16/09 with Olivia Munn- it was rated number 3 in Coolest College Classes; and Stacy Conradt and author John Green from 26 Bizarre College Classes on Mental Floss YouTube, 11/6/13, 1.78 MM views (I had three courses in this list).

Thanks to Nicola Householder for graphic design consultation.

Gratitude for three great professors I had while attending University of Minnesota: Ron Libertus (1938-2018) American Indian Art; Collins Oakgrove (1944-2014) Ojibwe Language and Culture; and Tom Conley, Film.

All of the proceeds from the first edition were donated for health, 45% of the second for education, and 40% of the third for both of the aforementioned and animal welfare.

Library of Congress Cataloging-in-Publication Data
Russo, Ron.
Adult swim and comedy/Ron Russo. - Fourth ed. p. cm.
ISBN 978-0-9771377-5-6   LCCN 2018907747
Copyright 2005, 2008, 2012, 2019 Fourth edition.
Published by Gai Russo, Inc.
P. O. Box 38, Chagrin Falls, OH 44022
gairusso.com/shop/adult-swim-and-comedy
Cover: *The Little Girl Who Killed Your Cat.* by Angus Oblong.

Introduction

This edition is a centennial celebration as I just finished teaching my 100th upper division college Comedy course, thirty-seven of them being Adult Swim.[1] Three years after the network's launch, in the Fall of 2004, I started the world's only Adult Swim course.

The network has been super kind to the class, from Jim Babcock in Marketing occasionally sending the students swag for hands-on analysis, to a fifteen year record where not one executive or show creator has ever turned down a request to volunteer their time. We've been fortunate enough to have the following nine VIPs for class teleconference events: 2004-Brendon Small, and Mike Lazzo and Keith Crofford; 2006-Tim Heidecker and Eric Wareheim; 2007-Dave Willis and Matt Maiellaro; 2012-Jon Glaser; and 2017-Seth Green. In 2014 Tim and Eric (and John C. Reilly) provided complimentary seats, fourth and fifth row center, for the entire class to their sold-out performance at the Ohio Theater. In 2015 Angus Oblong travelled from Los Angeles to speak with the class. He has been a stalwart supporter of the textbook, illustrating all four book covers, adding a chapter and illustrations to the past three editions, and even supplying Oblong font for part of the text here. He's also the funniest person I know.

Television and online programming are constantly changing mediums; most of the work herein can be updated on a daily or weekly basis. Why do some shows only get a mention or two and not a full article? I'm a one-man band and each article takes from one to eighteen weeks to write. It's always a case of just running out of time, even for some of my favorite shows. According to Joe Pera, a teacher character on Adult Swim, "Working at my usual pace it would take me ten years to finish."[2]

Adjunct Professor Ron Russo, Kent State University,
Department of Journalism and Mass Communication.

---

[1] I have two more world's only Comedy courses, Adam Sandler and Will Ferrell. I've also taught 62 Film and 10 Art courses.

[2] "Joe Pera Talks To You About The Rat Wars of Alberta, Canada (1950-Present Day)," 6/11/18.

Reclamation Part 1

"Home Movies," 1999-2004.

Creators Brendon Small and Loren Bouchard.

"Home Movies" is a trend-setting animated TV series (picked up and then) produced by Adult Swim. Different lineups of the creators and cast go on to be main cogs in half a dozen TV shows, two live-action and four animated: "Jon Benjamin Has A Van," "Delocated," "Lucy, the Daughter of the Devil," "Archer," "Metalocalypse," and "Bob's Burgers." This makes "Home Movies" the starting point for one of the largest and most influential comedy blocks of the century.

Comedians have historically been voice actors in animation but not to the extent of "Home Movies." Three of the original four cast members are comedians: Brendon Small, H. Jon Benjamin, and Paula Poundstone The latter was a stand up headliner in the late 90s. She was, in part, cast for this role as a single mother because that was a prominent aspect of her personal life (actor/character conflation). Her animated character used her real first name and near regular voice, just like Brendon Small and Melissa Galsky.

More comedians surround the main cast in cameos or recurring roles. Mitch Hedberg (1968-2005) appeared in four episodes of the first season of "Home Movies." His distinct low level voice, occasional slow or drawn out pronunciation, and cadence made him a natural for animation. If you extract the curse words from his solo material, most all of it would be rated G, General Audiences for all ages; this is not that common as most comics rely on adult situations. Mitch does four characters in "Home Movies" but his namesake Mitch, the cool fifth grader in "Yoko," 1999 is noteworthy, "It's going goood, ... yeah I put an extra 'O' in the good, cause it's so good!" A recurring Russian ethnic/national student Eugene (Mirman) premieres in "Yoko," he speaks the following infamous line in a heavy accent, "I pee in Coach McGuirk's canteen ... it is practically joke."[1] The Eugene Mirman Comedy Festival ran in NYC for a decade, 2007-17, and included many popular comics-some his cast costars.

UPN cancelled "Home Movies" only five episodes into its first season and

---

[1] Eugene Mirman, born in Moscow, plays another Russian character (Yvgeny) ten years later in the live-action "Delocated." Sacha Baron Cohen's Borat Sagdiyev was from the neighboring country of Kazakhstan, and an earlier character model also from the Caspian Sea area was Andy Kaufman's Latka Gravas of "Taxi," 1978-83.

Adult Swim then picked it up and produced 47 more. "Home Movies" kicked off the official launch of Adult Swim on 9/2/2001. After season one, Soup2Nuts quit using its trademark squigglevision, where five similar but slightly different drawings were run in loops to produce a vibrating effect. This Boston based company does all of its work in-house; a great business model that facilitates creative control. To save time and money the sets are color-block sketches with limited detail. The characters, too, are in single color outfits that cover their hands and feet. Brendon's outfit is blue and his backward spikes of orange hair balance his figure against his long Pinocchio nose (he mentions the wooden boy while cloud watching in "The Wizard's Baker," 2004). It is common in animation that the characters and story line intertwine with fables. The partly improvised audio recording sessions of "Home Movies" ran four to five hours and were edited down to show length, about 22 minutes.

Two of the five main characters in "Home Movies" were female, and voiced by females. Three of the five main characters in "Bob's Burgers" are female but only one, Louise, is voiced by a female, Kristen Schaal. All five voice actors of "Bob's Burgers" are comics! John Roberts has a wonderful YouTube back catalogue of his drag character named Mom. The voice and characteristics became the mother Linda on the show.

Brendon Small was not the only musician in "Home Movies" as Loren Bouchard helped cowrite many of the songs. Loren now has the characters from "Bob's Burgers" performing episode specific original songs in the closing credits; it has become one of the show's identifying trademarks.

"Bob's Burgers" breaks new ground because the main set is a restaurant; there is little precedent for this in either animation or sitcoms. At Halloween, several restaurants across the continent (Chicago, Pittsburgh, Vancouver, and NYC) have transformed into Bob's Burgers with costumed employees serving burgers featured on the daily special blackboard. "Bob's Burgers" has a few burger recipe books, comic books, branded games, and a new film for theaters set for release in July 2020! H. Jon Benjamin released his comic autobiography *Failure is an Option* in May, 2018. He has a great 45 minute discussion on the book with cohost Eugene Mirman at the Strand Bookstore in NYC.[2] Eugene and H. Jon, along with other former "Home Movies" cast members, have been working together for almost 20 years: the closing scene of "Yoko," 1999 has fourth-grader Eugene yelling in pain as an adult Coach McGuirk repeatedly hits him with soccer balls.[3]

---

[2] 13 May 18, "H Jon Benjamin & Eugene Mirman | Failure is an Option." YouTube, uploaded by The Strand Bookstore.

[3] Melissa Galsky has done about 20 episodes of voice acting on "Bob's Burgers," Brendon a few. Melissa and Holly Schlesinger have worked in production for both shows, too.

"The Oblongs," 2001-02.
Creator Angus Oblong.

As a youngster in his early twenties Angus' book *Creepy Susie and 13 Other Tragic Tales for Troubled Children* was nominated for The 1999 Bram Stoker Award in Work for Young Readers category. He was beat out by then new author, J.K. Rowling. Angus did, though, get to personally deliver that year's Lifetime Achievement award to Edward Gorey's surviving relative (he died after his nomination). Stephen King and Neil Gaiman were also nominees in other categories that year. Warner Bros. signed both Angus and Rowling and their respective WB works were released in 2001: "The Oblongs" animated TV series, and *Harry Potter and The Sorcerer's Stone*.

Angus' *Creepy Susie and 13 Other Tragic Tales for Troubled Children.*, 1999 is a collection of short stories that were originally self-published. Each of the 14 stories are between three, *Emily, Amputee.*, and sixteen, *Stupid Betsy.*, pages in length. Each page has a single black-and-white illustration that is often accompanied by a single sentence of hand lettered text. The style could not appear more simple and straightforward; yet there are advanced art and comedy elements at work. In *Stupid Betsy.* each of the 16 illustrations are contained in their own unique picture frame. The ornate frames are one of the author's signatures that can also be seen with his photo in the back of the book, and carry over to the walls of the TV series. His use of the period and ellipsis in text creates a distinct form of writing. The illustration of Stupid Betsy on page 21 has her staring at the reader sitting on the edge of her bed, and the headboard protrudes out of the picture frame. Her outstanding costume element is a pair of bunny slippers, and there are two interesting props (an Oblong speciality) on the floor: an unplugged electric toaster laying on its side, and a single marble with shadow (on page 19 it is established that she has an unusual problem with them). The two fangs show Stupid Betsy has just turned into a vampire and through the German Expressionist crooked window we see a bat against a full moon in long shot. The static illustration depicts movement in the "blowing" curtains.

Another tale, *Dick and Muffy.,* is 13 pages of visual (no dialogue or text) double entendres. Many of "The Oblongs" TV characters were pulled from these short stories: Helga, The Debbies, Milo, Creepy Susie, etc. Other traits seen in both the TV and print versions are as follows: many of the characters have no noses and all have only three fingers (both common traits in animation); signature breasts, such as four on the school nurse and one on Peggy; oblong floor shadows that resemble the bases for small plastic cast characters; and many pencil necks.

Angus began as an indie publisher in San Francisco. Historically, the 1970s underground comic book movement launched there and its pages provided the first "storyboards" for adult cartoons. The comic books were considered improper mainstream material of the era, but they were not marked with any rating or explicit warning. The San Francisco-Berkeley area had indie publishers Rip Off Press and Last Gasp. From the latter came *Slow Death*.[1] Like Adult Swim, it was a compilation of shorts from various author/illustrators, including R. Crumb. Gilbert Shelton was a contributor and had his own comic *The Fabulous Furry Freak Brothers*. Mike B. Anderson, with "The Simpsons" since its inception and now supervising director, was involved with a claymation film based on issue #5 of this comic, *Grass Roots*, 1977, but it has been stalled in production.[2] Angus and Mike were guests on an epic live stream with *The Obscenesters*, Lenora Claire and Dee Simon, in 2013. Mike worked with Angus on three projects: as producer for "The Oblongs"; actor and opening montage DOP for *Deliriously Jen* (2005); and director for the unreleased documentary on Angus, *Clown and Pig*.

Two of the tales in *Creepy Susie and 13 Other Tragic Tales for Troubled Children.* are titled after dogs, *Waldo and Bean.* and *Narcoleptic Scottie.,* and most of them contain either live or dead animals: cats, fish, rabbits, fowl, rodents, insects, and pigs. A pig is seen in an odd setting twice in *Rosie's Crazy Mother.*: first in a fish tank in midground of a crowded deep focus illustration, and then in a birdcage in a three shot. Going back to one of Angus' self made books, *Beanpole Betty.*, on page 2 there is an adorable sleeping pig, but, Betty is holding a wobbly tower of a pillow, blanket, pot, book, pail, bust, and chainsaw over it. In "The Oblongs: Disfigured Debbie," a young farmer is holding a pig that ends the scene with four oinks and a squeal. Angus' first pig was The Countess, and his current is Pugsley.[3] In "Narcoleptic Scottie" there is a turtle Boxy, and Angus' newest friend is rescue turtle Zooma Melvin Oblong.

Concurrent with the 70s underground comic book movement is Gonzo journalism. *Rolling Stone* magazine was also located in San Francisco for its

---

[1] Lastgasp.com/alg. It was originally created as an ecological not-for-profit comic and was released on the first ever Earth Day, 1970.

[2] The film also had grass roots fundraising as individuals could purchase film frames and have their name inscribed on them.

[3] Angus Oblong is often compared to Charles Addams, the *New Yorker* cartoonist. The 60s sitcom "The Addams Family" was based on his work; over the decades the show branched into other formats as both an animated TV show and a live-action film series. Pugsley was the name of the son, and the girl on the cover of this book recalls daughter Wednesday.

first decade, 1967-77. Ralph Steadman, famous English artist and illustrator, teamed up with infamous American journalist Hunter S. Thompson to create 35 years of unique work, much of it for this magazine.[4] With more text and a larger format the illustrations became more developed than their comic book counterparts being published as books, too, such as *Fear and Loathing in Las Vegas*, 1971, they could reach a much larger audience of young adults. Their Gonzo work could be considered the animatic to the underground comic books' storyboard.

Great minds, of different generations, think alike. The first page of Ralph's *Gonzo the Art,* 1998 has a polaroid close-up of his hand with the word NO painted across the palm; the final page is a polaroid head shot, titled *Self-Paranoid,* that has half of his face in clown makeup. Angus' primary character Milo Oblong always wears a NO. tee-shirt; and Angus always appears in public in clown makeup.

The voice cast includes the following comedians: Lea DeLaria as Helga, Pam Adlon as Milo, and Will Ferrell as Bob Oblong. Per Angus on Swim.com boards 8/27/11, "... occasionally Will would be in NYC doing SatNight Live, so he would be recorded via a phone line." Many SNL cast members work as voice actors in animation including Kate McKinnon, Aidy Bryant, Fred Armisen, Bill Hader, Andy Samberg, and Norm Macdonald as Pigeon in "Mike Tyson Mysteries." Items from Will Ferrell's trademark SNL skits will be blended into his characters throughout his career, sustaining his brand, even in animation. One character stream is seen in "Bucketheads" where balding Bob Oblong sings and plays *Puff the Magic Dragon* on a keyboard at Milo's middle school to an unreceptive audience. This originates with his earlier SNL recurring character, balding Marty Culp, the Alta Dena Middle School music teacher who sings and plays keyboard at mandatory school assemblies.

Another stream originates from Will Ferrell's scantily clad SNL recurring characters: life drawing art class model Terrance Maddox, and hot tub enthusiast Professor Clarvin. His one-off SNL character Dale McGrew wears only a thong and half shirt, both in a USA flag motif, with running shoes, to a meeting because he took an office memo on work attire literally, "little items to show our patriotism." Dale is thrown out of the meeting, invading the physical space of female coworkers to the end. In "Please Be Genital," Bob Oblong, wearing only his white briefs, has a disagreement with Pickles at home; he is also thrown out (a Ferrell trademark) then chased down the street by

---

[4] Their first project, though, was for *Scanlan's Monthly* in May, 1970, working on the article, *The Kentucky Derby is Decadent and Depraved* (Kent State is mentioned in it). Per Ralph's *Gonzo The Art,* 1998, pgs. 10-11, "**Gonzo** is the essence of irony. You dare not take it seriously. You have to laugh. Nobody I have read knows what GONZO is, was, or ever could be, not even Hunter, and if he doesn't know what it is, I do.... GOnzo makes you feel GOod rather than BAd which is BANZO ...." The term can be found in most dictionaries.

neighborhood dogs (there are no running shoes as Bob has no feet). Will Ferrell's key costume element while running around the racetrack "on fire" in *Talladega Nights: The Ballad of Ricky Bobby* (2006) is, again, his white briefs and running shoes (with white socks), racing helmet and gloves, and gold lightning bolt necklace.

Physical characteristics humor is a signature element of "The Oblongs." Predecessor Mister Magoo, whose eyes are closed 95% of the time, is often pleasant like Bob Oblong, but it is only him, not an entire family, Milo's friends, and even pets with severe physical and mental abnormalities (read Angus' *My Advice and My Story.* for his character descriptions). Angus' unreleased film *Amp* likely contains similar humor.

A common literary and film technique, entry/exit has similar shots to open and close a piece. *Deliriously Jen* uses two slapstick with foley shots: a wooden board hits her in the face, with foley, to open; and to close-a spin on the Jacques Tati whistle and pole gag from *Mon Oncle* (1958) FR-someone honks a car horn at Jen just as she is approaching a streetlight pole, she turns her head to acknowledge and runs face first into the pole, with foley.[5] The pole has an Oblong face drawn on it as did the bathroom wall in the opening scene. The test of time is a great barometer for a prank, though Jen's is staged, with some luck you can replicate the streetlight results right now, 60 years later.

In a global media market, books, TV shows, and such can be a hit in any given country. See the international group that sports Angus Oblong tattoos in Fan Stuff at his website, angusoblong.com. You can read movie reviews and purchase original artworks or prints, some with a special services option. Also see Appearances and if there is one nearby, go and meet him.

Angus, like many top Adult Swim creators, is skilled in multiple formats. He was the creator and writer of the play, *The Victorian Hotel.*, 2006. It included live actors, life size puppets, and animation. A dozen years later, theater troupes are still performing it. Angus' claim to fame is as an author and illustrator, so expect *The Victorian Hotel.*, *Creaky Heights.*, and an as of yet untitled compilation to be released as books soon. For the latter two, Angus recently posted a few teaser illustrations on Instagram!

"The Oblongs" may hold at least one record at Adult Swim because it was on its schedule almost year-round for quite awhile; possibly it has played this single season half hour show more than any other. Adult Swim was the catalyst for putting both "Family Guy" and "Futurama" back into production, a more Angus Oblong "The Oblongs" should be next.

---

[5] Sylvain Chomet's animated film *The Illusionist* (2010) FR/UK is based on an unfilmed Jacques Tati script.

"Mission Hill," 1999-2002.

Creators Bill Oakley and Josh Weinstein.

"Mission Hill" was a staple of the early Adult Swim line up but it has not been in the rotation for a few years. It was probably the apex of the older model, million dollar per episode, half hour animated shows. Warner Bros. animated only 13 of the 18 written episodes.

An excellent title theme song performed by Cake is accompanied by the images of the following five cast members: one female roommate-Posey; one male roommate-Jim (voiced by comedian Brian Posehn); the two costar brothers-Kevin and Andy; and the dog-Stogie. The latter is in all 13 episodes, unlike most other animated family pets who appear only when needed by the story line. For this reason the animators have done some research and made him a more detailed character: Stogie has the exact gait of a big Labrador Retriever with the characteristic side to side head wobble and tail wag, a trait found in some Labs.

Four supporting cast members live in the same apartment building: a couple, Wally and Gus, that provided TV's first animated gay kiss; and an artist/activist couple with a child. Unlike many other Adult Swim shows where the creators do voices for the main characters, here it is only for small recurring roles: Bill is George Bang; and Josh, providing the target for nerd and weight humor, is Toby.

"Mission Hill" employs a lot of implied line animation (lines that suggest direction, motion, and contact but in real life either can't be seen or are barely discernable) and it is immediately evident in the titles, accenting all of the characters' movements. Animators reduce the challenging hazy items, like cigarette smoke or steam from a cup of coffee, down to broken white lines of road lanes. In "Stories of Hope and Forgiveness" the implied line becomes surreal: Andy is mad at Kevin and his sightline directed at him literally becomes a barrage of small daggers, with accompanying foleys.

The slapstick fights between the brothers, some of the best ever done, are also evident at the close of the title sequence.[1] I tried to do a hit count for a sibling fight scene from the pilot and even at 1/8 slow motion there are still

---

[1] Study any work from the live-action The Three Stooges to understand slapstick with accompanying foley. The slapstick slowed down a bit in their later years, so pre-1957. Most of the terms from this comedy glossary are exhibited in any single The Three Stooges' work. *Can the Three Stooges Save the NBA?* 4/30/01 is an article from Hunter S. Thompson's *Hey Rube,* pgs.64-66, 2004.

too many, and a lot of implied line, for a definitive count. I'm guessing on average four hits per second.

The 2D "Mission Hill" and Eddie Murphy's concurrent stop-motion "The PJs," set in Chicago, both showcase urban realist sets with trash, empty bottles, peeling paint and such. Older brother Charlie Murphy (1959-2017) costarred in the live-action "Black Jesus." Its sets, too, feature urban realism in Compton with Lloyd being homeless. "Mission Hill" immediately brings to mind the name of a well-known neighborhood in San Francisco, the Mission (this area, though, is known for its lack of hills, and long time residents claim there are no overt references). In contrast, the Martin Denny-esque closing credit music by Eric Speier, the diner, the computer economy, and the stylistic and story line influence of 70s San Francisco underground comic books, suggest at least a hybrid of the Mission to this mid westerner.

"Mission Hill" employs several film elements such as mise-en-scene (a seemingly innocuous object of the set, for example, a fan, a light fixture, or a knick-knack that provides narrative, autobiographical, historical, or other information). In the opening shot of "Stories of Hope and Forgiveness" Kevin says to Andy, "This could be a bad day, a very bad day" and behind him is a black grated window fan that has a small chain hanging from it (there is actually a continuity break in this scene as the chain is missing from the fan in a few shots). A later street scene features several black ironwork window grates. These set pieces, and supporting dialogue, are a tip as to what will follow in the story line, Andy becomes handcuffed, i.e. the small chain, to a black ironwork fence for the remainder of the episode, over nine minutes.

Deep focus humor is also seen in this episode. Gus and Wally are in the foreground watching TV, and unbeknownst to them, through the window in the deep of the frame is a distant, small in size, Toby waving frantically as he is being chased by a rabid dog. A reframing of this shot in high angle is seen later with Kevin in the foreground watching TV and in the deep Toby still waving for help with the rabid dog in pursuit.

After this the creators did a sitcom with a similar premise to "Mission Hill," two roommate brothers living on their own, and it met the same fate, early cancellation. The two creators, as "The Simpsons" veterans, then returned to work with Matt Groening, but on "Futurama."

Reclamation Part 2

"Family Guy," 1999-2002 and 2005 to present.

Creator Seth MacFarlane.

"American Dad!," 2005 to present.

Creators Seth MacFarlane, Matt Weitzman, and Mike Barker.

"The Cleveland Show," 2009-13.

Creators Seth MacFarlane, Richard Appel, and Mike Henry.

A tale for those of you attending college: a 10 minute film for a school project parlays itself into a $100 million dollar animation contract (and worth a lot more now).[1] Seth MacFarlane made *The Life of Larry* (1995) while a student at Rhode Island School of Design. It stars the animated Cummings family that is basically the Griffins minus Meg and Stewie. The Dad Larry has the same voice and character as Peter but is much smaller in stature; the Mom Lois has the correct name but a different look and voice; the son Milt physically resembles Chris; and the dog Steve has the same voice and character as Brian but dissimilar in looks (see *Larry and Steve* in Color Art).

Seth acts as the live-action host of the animated film and states, "Keep an eye out for the outrageous 'Star Trek' parody." Larry and Steve are then shown watching "Star Trek" on TV. Captain Kirk moves in a herky-jerky fashion and eventually splits the seam of his pants. Eight years later in 2003, "Family Guy: When You Wish Upon a Weinstein," the 50th episode not shown on FOX, premiered on Adult Swim. William Shatner performs *Fiddler On The Roof* on stage and he moves in a more pronounced herky-jerky fashion. "Star Trek" takes up about three minutes of *The Life of Larry*, situated in the beginning, middle, and end with the last animation a long shot of the Starship Enterprise.

The Life of Larry displayed Seth's comic versatility: two sexual humor jokes; religious humor at Sunday mass; political humor/surrealism with a beer tap

[1] *The Wall Street Journal: The Family Guy Goes Online,* 9/5/08, W12, John Jurgensen. Seth and Shatner worked together on "The Comedy Central Roast: Charlie Sheen" 9/19/11.

inside Newt Gingrich's head; four ethnic/national humor scenes (three live-action Asian layered with socioeconomic humor, and one English); foleys of punches and breaking glass-not carried over into his half hour shows; film/TV parodies including *West Side Story* (1961), *Philadelphia* (1993), "Jeopardy!" and "Star Trek"; literal speech; gross out humor; and more.

Larry's final gag in the film is a fart joke. Ten years later, Peter's final gag in the film *Stewie Griffin: The Untold Story* (2005) is a fart joke (what type of joke a comic ends their act with is important). In the spin-off, "The Cleveland Show: Gone With the Wind," 2010, there are approximately 57 farts in 20 minutes, minus title/credits, in all probability a prime time TV record.[2] So, you start with an idea in college and build on it as your career progresses. Phew.

Seth is also a fan of other types of gross-out humor. In "8 Simple Ways To Buy My Teenage Daughter," 2005 all of the males in the family join in a lengthy vomiting contest; in just over a minute, they vomit 20 times. In "Quagmire's Dad," 2010 Brian vomits for 30 seconds straight. And for just the right balance of gross-out humor see "Brian and Stewie," 2010 where a dog and a baby with one diaper are locked in a bank vault for an extended period of time; the story plays out realistically. Yuck.

The opening shot of *The Life of Larry* is a one minute live-action long take of a wealthy Seth, later to become the animated Carter Pewterschmidt, talking condescendingly from a leather easy chair. "Family Guy" is one of the few shows on TV that regularly incorporates long take humor. In "Family Guy: Trading Places," 2011 we watch, via a single camera for an uninterrupted 90 seconds, Mr. Pewterschmidt learn how to operate a loader excavator just so he can smash a bus bench. Another 70 second long take with heavy equipment is seen in "Peter Problems," 2014; Peter on a forklift destroying, instead of saving, a beached whale.

On Seth's working method, "With the characters that I voice myself, the voice kind of always came first and the character design came afterwords."[3] Seth voices many characters in "Family Guy": Peter, Stewie, Brian, Quagmire, Tom Tucker, Mr. Pewterschmidt, and more. So in many scenes, he is acting against himself. Alex Borstein of "Mad TV" became the voice of Lois as "Family Guy" was originally slated to be a short within the show. This was the design for "The Simpsons" success as it was first an animated short on a comedy sketch TV show, "The Tracey Ullman Show," 1987, and members of its cast became the voice actors.

Seth Green of "Robot Chicken" is the voice of son Chris, whose Evil Monkey turns into his Stoopid Monkey productions and the logo includes the voice of

---

[2] *The Making of The Cleveland Show: Gone With the Wind* (n.d.) is an informative short.

[3] "Inside The Actors Studio," 9/14/09, Bravo TV.

Chris. Seth G. worked with Mila Kunis, sister Meg, in 2003-4, in "That '70s Show" as Mitch. He shares a family trait with his father Peter as their mouths are shaped like upside down frogs (turn your head a little and you'll see it). Both Seth M. and Seth G. have done *Star Wars* trilogies with their respective shows. Each episode of the "Family Guy" trilogy ends with an argument between the two show creators in their roles as Chris, "Yeah, but didn't 'Robot Chicken' already do this three months ago?" and Peter, " . . . I don't think people are even aware of that show's existence."

The Life of Larry was, again, both live-action and animated, and Seth's film series *Ted* is a similar mix. Ted's live-action spouse Tami-Lynn is played by actress Jessica Barth. She is a leader of the #MeToo movement, of course having nothing to do with Seth's films, as he has been outspoken on the subject for years. Glenn Quagmire will receive his comeuppance in a 2019 "Family Guy" episode.[4]

The character name Steve from "American Dad" may come from *Larry and Steve* (1996), the sequel to *The Life of Larry*. It was entirely animated, and the mom and son were omitted in favor of a guy and dog comedy duo. The Quagmire character is in it with the same voice, looks, and occupation as an airline pilot, but he goes unnamed. "Family Guy" character interactions begin here as the pilot, aka Quagmire, is mean or the proponent of slapstick to Steve, aka Brian, having him on the nose of the plane when it crashes.

Seth does the two lead voices on "American Dad," Stan Smith and Roger. The latter is an alien like Gazoo from the first prime time cartoon "The Flintstones," 1960. Stewie is modelled closely after Gazoo in both looks, a very large misshapen head on a toddler size body, and voice, an intelligent English accent. Seth was set to relaunch a new "The Flintstones" in 2013 but negotiations fell through. Seth's love of this show can be traced back to his childhood. His Dad Ron donated a drawing of Fred Flintstone made by a six year old Seth to the third edition of this book. *Larry and Steve* was also produced by the same 60s company as "The Flintstones," Hanna-Barbera. The "Star Trek" influence seen in his college project has, twenty-two years later, come full circle with Seth's live-action space series on FOX "The Orville."[5]

---

[4] *Huffington Post: "Family Guy "Character Will Have Me Too Moment, Producers Say. 7/21/18, David Moye. The Hollywood Reporter: Seth MacFarlane, 'Family Guy' Called Out Weinstein, Spacey, Ratner and Rose Before Sexual Misconduct Claims. 11/22/17, Ryan Parker.*

[5] Tim and Eric, Don Hertzfeldt, and others have released some great college work, too. New episodes of "Family Guy" premiere on FOX, and "American Dad" on TBS, and follow only days later on Adult Swim, an uncommon arrangement. FOX even did some text bumps, per 1/3/10, "You probably think this is Adult Swim, but it's not, it's FOX." This was reversed in an Adult Swim bump on 7/30/18 during a break of "Family Guy: Big Man on Hippocampus."

"Futurama," 1999-2003 and 2007-13.

Creator Matt Groening.

Before "The Simpsons," either the 48 shorts for "The Tracey Ullman Show," 1987-90, or the first half hour episode in December, 1989, Matt was a well known illustrator and author. His *Life In Hell* books, calendars, and T-shirts were common place items in the lives of 18 to 30 year olds.

The title "Futurama" was inspired by the 1939 New York World's Fair exhibit of the same name. Its tagline was "World of Tomorrow." In "Futurama: Space Pilot 3000," 1999, Fry awakes at Applied Cryogenics in 2999 and a worker says to him, "Welcome to the world of tomorrow." Don Hertzfeldt has referenced it, too, with the *World of Tomorrow* animated short film series. Designed by Norman Bel Geddes, it was a giant model that forecast America's transportation network of the 1960s. The title sequence of "Futurama" resembles that model. This positive spin future outlook was not evident at the start of the TV show as one of the working titles for "Futurama" was "Doomsville." The latter is certainly more in line with Matt's earlier titles such as *Life In Hell*.

A pluralistic cast, Fry is literally a red, white, and blue young American male (jacket, shirt, and pants respectively); Professor Farnsworth, distant uncle, is a senior citizen; Amy Wong is a young Asian-American female; Hermes is Jamaican-American; Bender Bending Rodriguez Unit 22, manufactured in Mexico, is implied Hispanic-American; Leela is a human with the physical characteristic of one eye, her love interest is Fr(eye); and Dr. Zoidberg is an alien, a genre where mutations are standard. He is a topsy-turvy Jewish stereotype in that he is both a shellfish, an item which is forbidden to strict observers, and a terrible doctor for human patients, see "The Series Has Landed" where he thinks that Fry is a female and that he should have two mouths.

Leela is inspired by a character of the same name who appeared in the live-action English "Doctor Who" serials in 1977-78 (the show ran for 26 seasons, 1963-89 and was revived in 2005 to present). The Doctor is both a time and space traveller, a forerunner to Fry in this respect. Leela was the Doctor's unofficial security guard. Both of the Leelas are tough space women, wearing one thick bracelet, wedge boots, and similar double strap tank-style tops. The third costar of "Doctor Who" is K-9, a robot dog that was so popular he got his own spin-off show.

Bender is likely the most well-known animated robot, and a proponent of slapstick humor in "Futurama," a Robonic Stooge. One of his animated predecessors, Rosie, comes from another 60s show, Hanna-Barbera's "The Jetsons."

The interior of a spaceship cockpit provides a standard set for the banter of unusual characters. There are a plethora of long running TV and film series and serials based on space and or time travel: from 1930s *Flash Gordon*; 60s "Lost In Space" and "Star Trek"; 70s *Star Wars* including recent parody trios from Seth MacFarlane's "Family Guy," and also his live-action "The Orville," and Seth Green's "Robot Chicken," and also Stoopid Buddy Stoodios' "Titan Maximum"; to 80s *Back to the Future* into "Rick and Morty"; etc.

The main set of "Futurama," Professor Farnsworth's combination living quarters/business, has an unusual TV precedent. "Chico and the Man," 1974-78, was a sitcom that paired an old curmudgeon and a young adult male who work and live in an auto repair garage (i.e. Farnsworth, Fry, and their transportation business). A small hint to this reference is that Bender and Chico have the same surname, Rodriguez. Unlike Matt's earlier "The Simpsons," which is primarily a family home centered set, "Futurama" is primarily a friends workplace set, along the lines of "Harvey Birdman, Attorney at Law." I would guess there are five to one shows set in the future versus the past. Period pieces require some accuracy in reconstruction or they are glaringly anachronistic. Whereas no one knows what the future looks like.

The production cost per episode of "Futurama" fell somewhere in between "Home Movies" and "The Oblongs" at about $500,000.00. What is most eye opening is the price networks pay for the reruns. In 2002 Adult Swim purchased five-year cable TV rights of all five seasons of "Futurama" for ten million dollars, or 25% of the original production cost. At renewal Comedy Central outbid Adult Swim at 28.8 million, or 75% of the original production cost; it was last shown on Adult Swim in a New Year's Eve 2007 marathon.[1] The series finale, "Meanwhile," aired on 9/4/13.

"The Simpsons: Simpsorama," 11/9/14 on FOX was a great crossover, and unusual in that both shows were from a single creator. Matt's newest animated work is "Disenchantment," 2018 on Netflix. The voice cast includes three Adult Swim alumni: Noel Fielding; Eric Andre; and veteran Billy West (Mr. Klimer, James, and Anita Bidet of "The Oblongs" and Fry, the professor, and Dr. Zoidberg of "Futurama").

---

[1] *Variety: Animation Central: 'Futurama' in Comedy's future via big deal,* 10/27/05, John Dempsey.

"King of the Hill," 1997-2010.
Creators Mike Judge and Greg Daniels.

Let's track the inception of Hank and Peggy Hill from a two minute short in 1991, *The Honkey Problem*. The star, Inbred Jed, is the lead singer of a western swing trio, a forerunner to Hank in voice, accent, and dialogue with a few of the catchphrases, "good God" and "God damn." In the audience at this outdoor music performance is a woman who physically resembles Peggy but with gray, instead of brown hair and round, instead of square glasses; and a blond teenage girl in a half shirt who resembles Luanne (with a boy who only suggests Lucky).

Closer to Hank and Peggy Hill are Tom and Marcy Anderson from the feature film *Beavis and Butt-Head Do America* (1996). Tom talks about the butane gas regulator on his camper (Hank is a propane salesman) and several tag lines like the following: "You know," "Boy, I tell you what," "It doesn't get any better than this," or his yodel like frightened yell, "Augh, augh, augh!" Tom's costume is getting closer to Hank's with a white T-shirt, brown shoes, brown watch, blue bucket hat, and blue Bermuda shorts.

In "King of the Hill: Pilot," 1997 the progression is complete. Hank Hill's costume is Tom's if you lengthen the blue shorts to blue pants and add Inbred Jed's silver belt buckle. Inbred Jed and Tom Anderson both wear hats, and as Hank rarely wears one, the rectangular shape of his head became more defined. A major change is that both Hank and Peggy were made about 10 to 15 years younger than either of their two predecessors.

The opening title/credits of *The Honkey Problem* (1991) are scrolled across the back of a pick up truck that features its muffler/tailpipe and a Texas vanity license plate. In "King of the Hill: Pilot" there is a scene where Bobby and Joseph throw pebbles into Hank's tailpipe, and one shot from beneath the car includes the muffler. The final shot of this episode focuses on a Texas license plate as a bus drives off into the distance.

A specific Texas town is established in the opening shot of "Pilot" with the Arlen water tower. Regional weather is in the dialogue as Hank says to Dale, "We live in Texas, it's already 110 in the summer and if it gets one degree hotter I'm gonna kick your ass." Texas related items abound: in Bobby's room there is a stuffed armadillo, the state animal, and a Dallas Cowboys' pennant; the Texas State seal is seen on The Arlen County Child Protective Services building; and on their kitchen wall is a picture that resembles The Alamo.

A single "lone" star is on their beer cans but the brand name Alamo is not seen until episode two or three.

In *Beavis and Butt-Head Do America* (1996) Tom Henderson is constantly harassed and abused by government officials, ATF agents, and two young boys, Beavis and Butt-Head. Likewise for Hank in "Pilot" with a State social worker, and Bobby and Joseph. Another good methodology is to compare and contrast a pilot with its series finale, "To Sirloin With Love," 2009.[1] "Pilot" has Hank and Bobby attempting to bond over his participation in a school baseball game that includes fans in the bleachers. In the finale, Bobby wins the school a State Championship in meat judging with fans in the bleachers, and the father and son do overtly bond. In a flashback it shows Hank teaching a baby Bobby about cuts of meat. The finale also borrows from a famous early episode, "Life in the Fast Lane, Bobby's Saga" where Hank does not believe Bobby's judgement that his new boss Jimmy Witchard is crazy. In the finale it's his judgement of the senior meat graders. I'll get judgement in three consecutive sentences with the name of one of Mike's production companies, Judgemental Films. Also we can clearly see a "Judge" badge in the final scene of the meat grading.

There was some buzz that FOX was interested in reviving "King of The Hill" but nothing solid yet. The cast would be without two of its supporting voice actors: Brittany Murphy (1977-2009) was Luanne, and Tom Petty (1950-2017) was Lucky. The Cinemax animation "Mike Judge Presents: Tales From the Tour Bus" revolves around country music stars and relates directly back to *The Honkey Problem*.

In the following show's aired pilot, "Space Ghost Coast to Coast: Spanish Translation," 1994, Brak and Sisto sample a few lines of dialogue from Beavis and Butt-Head, or possibly a good imitation as Mike Judge is not listed in the credits. He does become a guest on the show in season three, "Sphinx," 1997.

Mike also made a commitment as the annual curator of *The Animation Show* (2003-08). Adult Swim has broadcast some of its compilations. It was a multiplatform venue with film tours, DVDs, online content, and included both up and coming and established animators. Its website stated that it was the first animation festival created and produced with animators at the helm. Further there was no limit on the amount of work you could submit, no submission or licensing fees, and it did not take any rights upfront.

---

[1] Four unaired episodes from this season were later aired in 2010 following the series finale.

The Animation Show (2003-08).
Featured Artist Don Hertzfeldt.

Mike Judge and Don Hertzfeldt were the copresenters of the first *The Animation Show*. Don's films were in three of its four programs. He is a breath of fresh air in the entertainment industry, a successful indie with high-end skills and principles.

His works are immediately identifiable-a great trait for an illustrator, artist, and or filmmaker. Don employs painstaking craftsmanship with his 1940s animation/titles camera. In his 17 minute film *Everything Will Be Okay* (2006) many of the effects are made to order, such as placing his drawings under a raised piece of glass and pouring water over it for a rain effect, or even chocolate syrup for an imagination shot. One of his signature elements is the use of multiple focal points in a frame. For example, there are eight separate screens of action in one frame while Bill is thinking about the futile and useless things he does repetitively every day: washing dishes, vacuuming, brushing his teeth, going to the bathroom, watching TV, flicking light switches, and two different shots of him with his keys. To achieve the multiscreen effect Don hand tears mattes from dark construction paper, places them an inch below the lens, and makes multiple camera passes. Many of these composite shots also mix in photos such as Bill and his ex-girlfriend lying down on the bottom of the frame, and an umbrella of real trees is across the top.

His working methods are explained in detail in the *Special Features* sections of his DVDs: there are 130 pages in *Everything Will Be Okay* and 148 pages in *I Am So Proud Of You* (2008). You maneuver through the menus by single page clicks, so you get a feel for some of the slow processes involved with animation, particularly traditional.

Don is well known for his 9.5 minute film *Rejected* (2000). It consists of TV promos and commercials that were rejected by networks and sponsors (for such things as a speech bubble with the following text, "I am a consumer whore!") that subsequently take on a life of their own. Don's subtitled commentary states, "I've turned down more money by refusing all real commercial work than I want to think about ... to me commercials are nothing but lies."

A featured methodology in this book is to track an artist's work from college to present. Don created the 5.5 minute short *Billy's Balloon* (1998) while a student at the University of California, Santa Barbara. Everything is in black-

and-white except for grey clouds and multicolored helium filled balloons. The cast are all toddlers so there is no dialogue, only sound effects. Billy's red balloon pummels him in implied line slapstick and then lifts him into the sky only to drop him to the ground. More children and balloons are shown, in multiplication, in the same scenario. Several of the sky drops are illustrated in long shot humor where the cast is very small in relation to the frame. Few artists use this technique on a regular basis.

Don's most recent work is the 23 minute *World of Tomorrow Episode 2: The Burden of Other People's Thoughts* (2017). The simple black-and-white characters carry forward but on magnificent multilayer color sets. Background music has been added with six classical music pieces, and indigenous music takes place with a brief piano and vocal duet by Emily 6 (Julia Pott) and Emily Prime (Winona Mae, aka Don's niece) in the Bog of Realism. There are several other great location names such as Triangle Land, and the Valley of Buried Memories, it recalls the locales in The Beatles' *Yellow Submarine* (1968) USA/UK, The Foothills of The Headlands, the Sea of Nothing, etc.

A mark of high quality dialogue is that you'll recall an audio clip of a character's line long after you've seen the work, sometimes forever! The black space image in Color Art has three multiples of Emily 6, the two on either end are speaking the following simultaneous, overlapping, lines of dialogue: Left "I was next in line to be Emily and now I am no one."; and Right "It's easy to get lost in here." The shot prior to this has three Emily Primes (multiplication) with the one on the right repeating "bracelet" twice (repetition)..

Don Hertzfeldt's characteristic skills have evolved over the years making *World of Tomorrow Episode 2: The Burden of Other People's Thoughts* (2017) one of the top films ever made, animated or otherwise.

"The Boondocks," 2005-14.

Creator Aaron McGruder.

"Black Jesus," 2014 to present.

Creators Aaron McGruder and Mike Clattenburg.

This show is in Reclamation Part 2 because the pilot was originally a FOX project. This is the first new Adult Swim show that began as a newspaper comic strip-a traditional model that includes Charles Schulz' *Peanuts* into Charlie Brown TV specials, or Hank Ketcham's *Dennis the Menace* into its animated and live-action TV shows and films.[1] "A Huey Freeman Christmas," 2005 relates to "A Charlie Brown Christmas," 1965 in title and name (the stars have the same long E second syllable ending, too); in song "Christmas Time Is Here" and similar piano background music in the style of Vince Guaraldi; and in story line, Huey the school play director is highly irritated by the cast dance scene. There is a large poster behind Huey at the school that says The Adventures of Black Jesus with a head shot illustration of Jesus; is this the origin of the subsequent show? The live-action TV series "Dennis the Menace," 1959-63, starring Jay North as Dennis and Joseph Kearns as Mr. Wilson, is the real blueprint for "The Boondocks," intertwining geezer (Granddad) and juvenile (Huey and especially Riley) humor. Neither of the aforementioned seniors, Mr. Wilson nor Granddad, are an actual parent. John Witherspoon, the voice actor for the latter, is a veteran comedian and is also in "Black Jesus" as Lloyd. Charlie Murphy (1959-2017) and Slink Johnson, both "Freaknik: The Musical" alumni, join John to comprise part of its main cast.

The geezer/juvenile mix is also seen in stand up comedy, for example, *Here and Now* (1983), one of only two films written, directed, and starring Richard Pryor. His geezer character Mudbone says, "Boy, tie your shoe," and the little boy answers back, "Go f##$ yourself" to which Mudbone replies, "I hope you fall on your ugly ass face." Another line from Mudbone, "I can still kick a little ass now and then" could be right out of "The Boondocks: Granddad's Fight."

The comic genre of cursing is much like slapstick. If you do an actual count, you'll be surprised at the large number. Each comic or comic character has

---

[1] Other Adult Swim shows from a newspaper comic strip include the reclamation "Baby Blues," and the new "The Drinky Crow Show" from *Maakies*.

his or her own identifiable group of curse words. Most episodes of "The Boon-docks" employ some cursing like "The Real" where Riley says to Granddad, " . . . when Xzibit brings that car back you gonna be bitches," and Granddad responds "What did you call me?" and later Huey replies to Riley, "No disre-spect? you just called your grandfather bitches," and on to where Granddad says his new full name, "Granddad Bitches Freeman, it's got a nice ring to it." In 35 seconds they say "bitches" seven times. Be aware, invariably, right after viewing, the curse words can work their way into your normal speech pattern due to their stand out quality, rate of occurrence, or just general human na-ture to mimic, and you could accidently call someone "bitches!"

It is great that some of the episodes raise awareness about social topics, in particular, "Invasion of the Katrinians." Though, Granddad was not inclined to lend assistance in the story line, voice actor John Witherspoon went to New Orleans in the aftermath to help fix up homes and do some comedy perform-ance fundraising. Not related to the show, then 19 year old Bow Wow donated 10% of the opening weekend proceeds of *Roll Bounce* (2005) to Operation USA For Hurricane Katrina. To my knowledge, not one of the other feature films that opened that weekend matched him. This latter fundraising method or an earmarked percentage of a media product's net, is the charitable entertain-ment model of the future (not Young Reezy's Fun-Raiser method). Further, another then 19 year old, Japanese golfer Ryo Ishikawa, donated his entire year tournament proceeds to earthquake/tsunami victims.[2] These young, and sometimes very old-sorry John, sports and entertainment professionals get it! There is hope for the future.

Preadolescent (about 9 to 12 years old) boy stars have a history of success in animation: Bart Simpson, Shin Chan, Meatwad, Orel Puppington, Rusty Cuyler, Charlie Brown, Milo Oblong, and Bobby Hill to name a few. Most of the aforementioned are voiced by women as are Riley and Huey Freeman, both by Regina King.

"The Boondocks" was primarily done in an anime style by Korean studios such as Lotto, Moi, and Dong Woo. One of the characteristics of this style is the long opening and closing credits; it is common for them to be about 90 seconds apiece, such as in "Cowboy Bebop." This is on average two to three times the length of American TV animation. "The Boondocks" titles and cred-its are only about 32 seconds apiece, but stylistically, its credits, and there are a few variations over the seasons, exhibit many anime traits: multiple fighting and action illustrations accenting implied line with weapons like a ninja

---

[2] Musician/comedian Bo Burnham, at about the same age of 19 in 2010, had some comic songs, "Art is Dead" and "Oh Bo," that address the economics of entertainment and an entertainer's social responsibility.

sword, a nunchaku, or a gun; a split or paralleled screen; an accented light source with big shadows; black silkscreen style stills; the character design elements of large eyes and a very small mouth with a tendency to show a pronounced spit or sweat; and a wide variety of camera angles (see camera placement in Film glossary) including oblique, much like a feature film. All of the aforementioned are also in-episode along with details such as an occasional smoking cigarette or black bird sighting. The only in-episode difference is the high quality of the Japanese audio track. Japan has led the way in audio with the still unsurpassed work of Osamu Tezuka's "Astro Boy," 1963 (English version-first anime/manga on US TV). The recent wave of anime series are redefining or expanding all of the aforementioned characteristics.

"Fooly Cooly" (FLCL) was a short lived six episode anime series aired in 2000-01. In 2018, seventeen years later, a new "FLCL: Progressive "(season 2) and "FLCL: Alternative" (season 3) aired on Toonami, the 10:30 PM Saturday night to 4 AM Sunday morning anime block of Adult Swim, currently hosted by TOM 5 and SARA 4. For FLCL continuity, the animated and live-action yellow Vespa from the original credits carries over but only animated. They've kept the same band, The Pillows, too, but with new songs. Per an online exclusive with the musicians at adultswim.com, they were not initially enamored with the original FLCL project as it was an unusual assignment, but it soon made them famous. Recently, "Dragon Ball Super" moved to 8 PM weeknights to open the regular Adult Swim block (two episodes of "Cowboy Bebop" closed out the first night ever of Adult Swim). "Attack on Titan," "My Hero Academia," "Naruto: Shippuden," "One Punch Man," "Hunter X Hunter," "Jojo's Bizarre Adventure: Stardust Crusaders" and more fill out Toonami.

"Pop Team Epic" is comic anime; somewhat of a sketch show format that builds on "Shin Chan" with multiple voices per character, more chapter breaks, and occasional inclusion of puppets, live-action, and storyboards. "Samurai Jack" is also different in that it is the only show on Adult Swim that is not dialogue driven. A theater screening of this show really highlights the visual artistry in its nature landscapes, including animals.

Williams Street produced eight episodes of a 15 minute anime parody "Perfect Hair Forever." The show was in English but Adult Swim did a one-off marathon with added subtitles purposely mistranslated to highlight national humor.

My Advice and My Story.
by Angus Oblong.

Hello. So I hear from Ron that you up and coming VIPs would like both some advice on how I "did it" and on what I do to create my masterpieces of fine, highbrow artwork.

My first chunk of advice is to not be afraid of getting your work out there and having no fear of your ideas and designs getting stolen or derived from. For years, I wrote and illustrated, showing only friends, thinking, "If I show my stories to the public, someone out there will copy my style and my voice." That's both a paranoid delusion and a justified fear. But to hoard your work will do you no good. Even though a few of my ideas and designs have been outright stolen, I have no regrets.

I started writing 13 short *Tragedies* and made photocopies of them in a local print shoppe. I stapled them together as individual booklets and sold them as a set (tied together with yarn) for $20.00. I was young. And looking back on pictures, my skin was damn good.

In the backs of these books, the reader could find my PO box and information on how to buy their own set of these self-published literary masterpieces. So, the more book sets I sold, the more I sold! It got to the point where I couldn't make them fast enough. Not out for more money, I didn't higher my prices, but found ways to make more copies for less cost; hundreds of books at a time. My one bedroom San Francisco apartment was littered with stacks of uncut copies, cover sheets, envelopes and yarn. A real chick magnet.

As happy as I was with their success, I wanted these books professionally published and on the shelves of bookstores. I shopped them around to local publishers, getting rejected every time. Maybe it was the cover letter I wrote in crayon (I thought that was charming) or maybe it was that their first glance (without their committing to reading a full story) was simplistic artwork- a small, round-headed character standing in the middle of an otherwise blank page with a single sentence hovering above their heads. I remember taking the advice of a customer of mine (I worked in a coffee house) and took my books in person to a publisher in the Mission District. Young and naive, I stood patiently while the large burly man flipped through one of my books, thoroughly unimpressed by what he saw. Upon looking closer to my atmosphere, I saw a lot of naked women. This place published . . . pornography.

"We don't do kiddy porn" said the burly man, handing me back my stack of booklets. I was mortified. Note to self, never listen to my f##$ing ass#%$$ customers.

"New York is where you want to publish," everyone told me. But I wanted a local publisher just in case I needed to barge into their offices, yelling and flailing my arms about something. What that might be, I had no idea, but the concept was a nice one. I was self-published with these books for five years.

I allowed a local agent to get me in touch with an agency in Beverly Hills where a friendly little bald agent named Howie took me on as his client. I loved Howie and trusted him immediately. "Create an animated series!" said Howie. "Those are very hot right now." And so I did, using the characters from my self-published books. "Can you get me published?" I asked Howie. My books were published within a week. That was how I knew I was represented by the right place. I got my first paycheck from Ballantine Publishing House for twenty thousand dollars! That day I called in rich to work.

Being fascinated with human deformities and overall misery, I created a show about a family of freaks whose last name was Smith. The pipe smoking 1950s-like father had no arms and legs, but was as happy and upbeat as any man could be. The mother was a drunk, pill-popping floozy who passed out on the couch before noon, was a horrible cook, a fairly good mother, and was always horny. She was horrible but hilarious (I knew that no actual children would be harmed during the making of this show, so it seemed okay if she locked one of her children in a box for a day then forget about it for a week). Conjoined brothers, a little boy named Milo (from my book *Milo's Disorder*) who had every possible traumatic childhood disorder and on every medication known to man, and lastly, an adorable little girl with a huge, grotesque growth jutting from the side of her head.

But the show wasn't about them. The viewer at home was to follow the daily routines of Milo's collection of social reject friends who all gathered in a club-house in his back yard every day after school. Partly to hide from bullies, but also to squash slugs and do other horrible random things. Milo's friends included Helga the ugly, fat, loud girl who loathed the Debbies. There was Peggy the Mutant, with one boobie and no lower jaw; she was the voice of reason in the group, often keeping them out of jail. Mikey Butts, whose large, floppy butt cheeks made him laughable, even to his friends and his neglectful family. And death obsessed Creepy Susie who floated a foot above the ground. Why? Hell, maybe she's possessed. I really didn't know. Milo and his friends were at the very bottom of the social hierarchy at school, only above the Girl with a Beak. They could pick on her and her only.

I had come up with many hilarious scenarios for Milo and his friends to get into, complete with illustrations to sell the Suits on the ideas once that bridge had to be crossed. "See? Look, Helga is stuck in a sewer pipe. Behind her, all of the town's poo is pressed into her backside. Maybe even poo could build up so much pressure, that it goes into her butt and out of her mouth! Hilarious, right?" In my mind, the Suits were laughing heartily at this idea. But my mind often proved to be different from the other kids.

Where I had gone wrong in my creation of this animated series was that it was underdeveloped. In my imagination, I was teamed up with other humans like me. They got my sense of humor and together we could flesh out this show, making it the best, and most hilariously offensive thing on network television!

I had created a show Bible- a bound book, filled with everything and every-one in the show. Character biographies, illustrations, the town, jokes, scenarios, episodes, etc. And so my agency made (badly) coloured copies and sent to every mildly interested studio in Los Angeles. What was happening? It was all very cool. I didn't need to eat ramen anymore!

My agent put me into a room with Bruce Helford to see if we got along. What was supposed to be a half hour meeting turned into over two hours of Bruce and I talking about cartoons, new characters, concepts and anything funny that would make a viewer at home cringe and laugh at the same time. I loved him instantly. Bruce was in.

We were represented by the same agency and sold as a united clump. The bidding war was on. My agency would update me on who was bidding the highest for "Unnamed Angus Oblong Project." In the end, it was down to FOX, Warner Brothers and Disney. I was so green, just having come from waiting tables at Mel's Diner in San Francisco, that I barely had any idea what was going on between agencies, networks and studios. Had I felt that I had a say in matters, I would have insisted we go with FOX due to their track record with prime time animation. But we seemed to be going with WB! That's fine. Bugs Bunny was with WB and Bugs Bunny was cool.

"What titles ideas do you have for your show?" an executive at WB asked me. "How about 'Peeing Into the Wind?'" I said with wide-eyed enthusiasm. He seemed ready for such a reply. "How about 'The Oblongs?' And we can name the family Oblong. It worked for Charles Addams!" I was floored. If I had one megalomaniacal bone in my body I had thought of it myself. And thus, "The Oblongs" were born.

I was not to be involved with the hiring of the writers. There were eight of us around the Writer's Table to solidify the story lines I had come up with. Bob gets animatronic arms and legs. Milo falls in love with an alien who dies tragically in the end. Helga's parents have been missing for two years and the kids find this out. This is going to be fun!

During the development stages, Bruce Helford was submersed in producing "The Drew Carey Show" and creating two other new shows, leaving me all alone. The writers and I did not share the same vision of the show. Ug. How. Frustrating. I stood up, walked out of the writer's room and never returned. I packed up and went to the animation house, Film Roman, where I knew an office waited for me.

I found myself amongst my people. An entire three floors of humans drawing "The Simpsons," "King of the Hill" and "The Oblongs!" I could wander around as they drew Bob, Pickles, Milo and Helga! And these people were genuinely happy for me in my new found position, no egos here. I designed characters, helped to shape backgrounds, created colour pallets and worked with the directors to make the show a visual treat.

There's really not much more to tell. It aired on WB for less than one season and then I read online that it had been cancelled. No. If my show had been cancelled, surely one of them would have told me, right? Welcome to Los Angeles.

I was both horrified and amused to hear that "The Oblongs" was yanked from the air in Australia in the middle of the first episode!

Luckily Adult Swim picked up the show and it found a second life. It was also released on DVD, which anyone who reads this should buy because that makes me just a little bit richer, which I'm sure makes you a little bit happier.

And that is my story. Go do the same. It was fun. Except for the parts that sucked.
Angus Oblong.

Williams Street : Recycled

The four inexpensive recycled shows below made up one-half of the original three hour Adult Swim block (now a 10 hour block). These 15 minute shows were produced partially or entirely in-house at Williams Street in Atlanta, home of Cartoon Network. This all began with Ted Turner's acquisition of the Hanna-Barbera cartoon library in 1991, with full control in 1993-94. As the largest cartoon library in the world with 147 TV shows, it needed to generate revenue aside from reruns on its sister station Boomerang.[1] Turner had previous success in this area in the mid 80s with the acquisition of the MGM/UA film library, colorizing select black-and-white films to create an additional revenue stream.

In 1994, Mike Lazzo brought in Keith Crofford and they created "Space Ghost Coast to Coast"; a recontextualized version of its first superhero, Space Ghost. It owned all of these 60s and 70s characters and could also save on production by recycling some of the original animation cels. By 2007, though, all four of the Adult Swim recycled shows were either cancelled or put on hiatus.

Schedule for Adult Swim Launch
Sunday, September 2, 2001

10:00 PM "Home Movies"
10:30 "The Brak Show" (recycled)
10:45 "The Brak Show" (recycled)
11:00 "Harvey Birdman, Attorney at Law" (recycled)
11:15 "Sealab 2021" (recycled)
11:30 "Space Ghost Coast to Coast" (recycled)
11:45 "Space Ghost Coast to Coast" (recycled)
12:00 AM "Cowboy Bebop"
12:30 "Cowboy Bebop"

---

[1] *The Art of Hanna-Barbera,* 1989, Hanna-Barbera /T. Sennett, 247-52, Viking Penguin. Origin of the name "Adult Swim" per Lazzo and Crofford 11/19/04: focus group parents chose it from three or four titles submitted by the On Air Department as it most identified adult material.

"Space Ghost Coast to Coast," 1994-2008.

Creators Mike Lazzo, Senior Executive VP; and Keith Crofford, Executive VP of Adult Swim.

The 1960s American/Russian space race fueled the space theme in numerous live-action TV sitcoms, from "My Favorite Martian," 1963 to "Lost In Space," 1965 and "Star Trek," 1966. Hanna-Barbera's TV animation led the way with "The Jetsons," 1962 and later followed up with "The Space Kidettes," 1966, "The Space Ghost," 1966, and "The Galaxy Trio," 1967. All of the HB shows premiered on one of the three free VHF networks of NBC, ABC, or CBS. This was also the time when the first version of alternate pay TV channels became the rage with UHF. The pay was a one time purchase of a special dial box that would give your TV usually an additional three channels, bringing the grand total to six. UHF provided some good alternative animation, like the Japanese "8th Man," and was in demand at households with children.

"The Space Ghost," 1966-68, not only premiered on a main channel but also had some of the highest ratings in the history of Saturday morning cartoons.[1] So Mike and Keith did not choose some obscure cartoon from the HB library to recycle but were banking on a proven star, though, a star who had been out of the limelight for almost 25 years. One of his arch villains, Zorak, too, had a hard time finding work after the show, and had to suffice with comedic roles. In "Jabberjaw: There's No Place Like Outer Space," 1976, Zorak appears in drag, complete with blue eye shadow, rouge, blonde wig, pink lipstick, and a laugh track.

"Space Ghost Coast to Coast" was put on hiatus for most of 2004 and all of 2005, his last appearance was a single starring role in "Perfect Hair Forever: Woke Up Drunk" and per the title the story line addresses his faultering personal life and career. His show returned for a few more seasons but was cancelled in 2008. In 2010 he appeared as a commercial spokesperson: on April Fools he and Moltar were with filmmaker Tommy Wiseau; and he and Steve Nash pitched Vitamin Water for that year's NBA Finals. As history repeats itself, the star is again out of the limelight, Will Space Ghost resume his show with a new staff (doubtful) or get a new show, and if so, will he be the same? C. Martin Croker (1962-2016) voiced both Zorak and Moltar, and his animation company Big Deal Cartoons worked on this and other AS shows.

---

[1] *The Art of Hanna-Barbera,* 1989, Hanna-Barbera /T. Sennett, 140-41, Viking Penguin.

Space Ghost certainly changed during his first absence. He abandoned his original support team of Jayce, Jan, and Blip and replaced them with two of his now enslaved arch enemies from The Council of Doom, Moltar and Zorak, a perfect dynamic for the classic office/workplace set where the employees and boss are antagonistic toward one another. "Space Ghost Coast to Coast" parodies both the talk show staff and guests. Talk show icon Johnny Carson provided the platform for many young stand up comedians. Space Ghost launched some cartoon comic careers, too, including Shark of "12 Oz. Mouse," Early of "Squidbillies," the entire cast of "Perfect Hair Forever," and almost "Aqua Teen Hunger Force" (see their article for more details). This was not new to Space Ghost, though, as he had many HB characters appear on his original 60s show, like Shazzan and Mightor, but none were debuts.

Adult Swim brought back the original voice actor for Space Ghost, Gary Owens, but he only did the second pilot. George Lowe became the new voice actor for Space Ghost and Andy Merrill transforms super villain Brak with a teenage voice.[2] Moltar, too, was not so menacing as he was shrunk in size. Zorak as the show's band leader begins the audio CD branch of Williams Street with "Modern Music for Swinging Superheroes," The Cartoon Planet Band, 1996. The new TV theme song features electric guitar and female vocal effects similar to the classic themes of "Lost In Space" and "Star Trek."

Recontextualizing an established icon for humor, the basis for "Space Ghost Coast to Coast" and all of the recycled shows, is seen in Dada artwork. Marcel Duchamp's *L.H.O.O.Q.,* 1919 is a miniature replica of Leonardo da Vinci's iconic portrait *Mona Lisa,* 1503-05 but with an added graffiti mustache and goatee. The letters "LHOOQ" when pronounced in its originating French language interpret to either the sound of a fart or the phrase "she's hot in the pants."

Reusing cels is a standard time saving/cost cutting practice in animation, but the level and ends to which Space Ghost was recycled is unprecedented. The horror-film TV hosts of the 60s provided the closest predecessor. Ghoulardi, the Cleveland host of "Shock Theater," 1963-66, would adulterate a film with a combination of the following: replace the dialogue with his own or that of an unknowing celebrity; change the background music; appear in the film by means of FX; and or would intercut his own newly filmed material. The very first regular season episode "Space Ghost Coast to Coast: Spanish Translation," 1994, parodies "Mystery Science Theater," a more recent version of Ghoulardi.

---

[2] I can hear George Lowe every day on the radio as he is the station announcer, promos and IDs, for WNCX Cleveland.

"The Brak Show," 2000-03.

"Brak Presents the Brak Show, Starring Brak," 2000. Creators Mike Lazzo and Keith Crofford.

My favorite Adult Swim product is "The Brak Show" Sing-a-Long Radio, a small blue plastic FM transistor in the shape of a vintage TV with antenna, that has a two-inch full color relief of Brak's face sticking out of the TV screen. Brak's mouth will open and close in synch to whatever is on the radio, from sports talk, Spanish language, to even lip synch of instruments (made famous by Jerry Lewis in the 60s). He looks the same but his voice/character change is completely unpredictable as the radio has no dial markings. This is the story of Brak, a Council of Doom member from "The Space Ghost," 1966-68, that was recycled into a singing suburban teenage cat-boy in the 90s.

The new Brak was based on a mix of successful 50s sitcoms: 181 episodes of "I Love Lucy," 1951-57 (Hispanic dad and musical son); 235 episodes of "Leave it to Beaver," 1957-63 (the mom, Beaver, and the suburban set); and a whopping 435 episodes of "The Adventures of Ozzie and Harriet," 1952-66 (musical son and star burst title). For the latter Ricky Nelson performed many in-episode original guitar and vocal songs, and some would be released to vinyl. Per his website, 15 of his songs charted in the Top 10 and a few were number 1 hits, "Travelin' Man," and "Poor Little Fool." Ricky Nelson also covered "The Christmas Song," 1944 in "The Adventures of Ozzie and Harriet: A Busy Christmas," 1956. Beaver, the lone nonmusical son of the above three, did start a band in real life called Beaver and the Trappers and had a few great singles including "Happiness Is Havin," 1966.

Brak started out his new musical career as part of a trio with Space Ghost and Zorak, they released the following three audio CDs: "Modern Music for Swinging Superheroes," 1996; "Space Ghost: Musical Bar-B-Que," 1997; and "Space Ghost: Surf-n-Turf," 1998. Brak went solo in 2000 with "The Brak Album." Per Keith Crofford, it only received some local air play in Atlanta. Adult Swim needed a more innovative and financially well endowed strategy to enter the national music market.

The archetype cartoon band trio was Alvin and the Chipmunks. Created in 1958, their second single was an original holiday song, "Christmas Don't Be Late." Per their website, it set a sales record with 4.5 million singles sold in seven weeks. They then received their own TV series, "The Alvin Show," 1961.

The Chipmunks, and later The Chipettes, are the benchmark in cartoon band longevity with multiple TV shows, films, and audio CDs.

Live-action musician/comedians have a history of gold and platinum holiday songs, too. The McKenzie Brothers, Dave Thomas and Rick Moranis of "Second City Television," 1976-84, and feature film fame, *Strange Brew* (1983) have, in their self titled audio CD, a holiday cover of "The Twelve Days of Christmas." They insert Canadian national lyrics with food, drink, and clothing, i.e. back bacon, beer, and toques. Thirty-five years later people still argue if the beer lyric is "six packs of 2-4" (a colloquialism for six packs of 24 beers) or "six packs of Tuborg" (a famous Canadian beer). Their further twist on the song is the pre and post roll humor. The cut is 4.75 minutes, but the song itself is only 2.5 minutes, leaving the comedy team a 90 second intro and a 60 second epilogue that includes more national elements such as the Canadian holiday, Boxing Day.

"Aqua Teen Hunger Force" released a holiday CD in 2009, "Have Yourself A Meaty Little Christmas." Meatwad teams up with recording artist Neko Case for the colorful, Christmas red and green, gross-out humor in "Santa Left A Booger In My Stocking." Carl, Shake, and a mariachi band join Meatwad with national humor in "Feliz Navidad": the title and some of the lyrics are in Spanish; and they list about a dozen Mexican food items, four with "the queso and a side of guac." Adult Swim was on the right track with this holiday CD because the 2009 Grammy for Best Comedy Album went to another Christmas release, Comedy Central's "A Colbert Christmas: The Greatest Gift of All!" it includes the Jon Stewart duet, "Can I Interest You in Hanukkah."

Most everyone in America is familiar with at least one of Adam Sandler's four part "Chanukah Song," 1996, 1999, 2003, and 2015 as they get annual holiday air play. Part Three was released as the closing credit song for his animated holiday film *Eight Crazy Nights* (2003).

The Beatles also expanded into TV animation with "Yellow Submarine," 1965, and its namesake 1968 film was rereleased in theatres in 2018. "The Archie Show" debuted in 1968 and this cartoon band made a major mark in music: per *The Plain Dealer: The Top 100 of the Sixties*, 1/9/70 The Archies' song "Sugar, Sugar" rated number eight for the entire decade of the 60s! [1] Hanna-Barbera's "Josie and The Pussycats," 1970-72 and "Josie and The Pussycats In Outer Space," 1972-74 generated four somewhat successful singles, an album, and a live-action film.

"The Dethalbum," 2007 by Dethklok, the cartoon band from Adult Swim's "Metalocalypse," premiered at number 21 on The Billboard Top 200, making it the highest charting death metal release ever. According to an 11/11/07 Adult

---

[1] The Archies follow-up hit "Jingle Jangle" rated number 43 in *The Top 50 of 1970*, 6 or 7/1971 (torn copy), and number 71 in *The Top 100 of 1970*, 1/1/71.

Swim bump, it sold over 92,000 copies in less than six weeks. "Dethalbum II," 2009 surpassed the original, premiering at number 15 and selling 45,000 copies in one week. Dethklok has their own song books, too, read more in "Metalocalypse."[2.]

Also in '07, Adult Swim premiered musician David Banner's pilot "That Crook'd 'Sipp." Set in Sweet Tea, Mississippi, it added both another regional southern show, joining North Georgia's "Squidbillies," and a very strong music star. The show never came to fruition but many items were carried over into "Freaknik: The Musical," 2010 (read more on this in Cartoonography).

Adult Swim has its own record label, Williams Street Records, headed by Jason DeMarco. There is a free music library at adultswim.com currently stocked with 36 albums including "ATL Remix" and the annual Adult Swim Singles programs by various artists. It is now showing seven music videos including "Superjail!" based "Winner," 2011 by Cheeseburger; Christy Karacas is both a band member and cocreator of the show. Another from the same year, though not currently on the site, is a "Venture Bros." based "Jacket" by Shallow Gravy (Hank, Dermott, and H.E.L.P.eR); Doc Hammer is both a band member and cocreator of the show, too. "Off the Air" also released in '11 and the Baltimore based visual and music collective is still on the air. "Run the Jewels X Rick and Morty: Oh Mama," 2018 is another music video now showing. RTJ coheadlined with Flying Lotus, Mastodon, DJ Douggpound, T-Pain performing "Freaknik," and others for the first ever Adult Swim Festival of comedy and music in Los Angeles, October 6-7, 2018.[3] See more live music in Live Stream Online Programming.

A truly unique piece in the annals of Adult Swim music is "The Mouse and The Mask," 2005 by Danger Doom (Atlanta luminaries Danger Mouse and MF Doom). Each of the 14 cuts is based on a specific Adult Swim show and incorporates one or both of the following: existing audio clips from the show, for example, "Sofa King" is named after and includes its scene from "ATHF: Video Ouija," 2004; and new lyrics, for example, from Brak and Zorak in "The Mask." The lone non Adult Swim song is "Mince Meat," a part of the tag line, "I'll make mince meat out of that mouse" from "Klondike Kat," 1963.

In choosing to recycle Brak, a cat, Adult Swim was wise to keep with the tradition of Hanna-Barbera as its first feature short at MGM costarred a cat, Tom of *Tom and Jerry* (1940) as well as its first animated TV show, Reddy of "The Ruff and Reddy Show," 1957. Though, five of Hanna-Barbera's first 21 animated TV shows costarred a cat, not one of them, Reddy, Jinks, Snooper, Top Cat, nor Punkin Puss, was musically inclined like Brak.

---

[2] ultimate-guitar.com/news, 10/10/07; 10/13/09; 12/22/09; and 1/12/11. Brendon Small has solo albums, too.

[3] Though, not performing at the festival, Adult Swim veteran mc chris (ATHF and "Sealab 2021") had a few explicit lyric holiday releases "F*##ing Up My Christmas," 2001 and "Evergreen," 2004.

"Harvey Birdman, Attorney at Law," 2000-07. Creators Erik Richter and Mike Ouweleen.

Hanna-Barbera launched "Birdman" in 1967, the year after its successful premiere of "The Space Ghost"; the former lasted for 40 episodes and the latter 60. Being a part of the same company, there are many similarities between the two superheroes. For their physical characteristics, both have cleft chins and no eyes, only white marks in the eye area of their masks. Their supporting casts are comprised of a pet, Avenger the eagle/Blip the monkey; and teenage assistants, Birdboy/Jan and Jayce. Both superheroes yell out their names while in flight, shoot rays out of their hands, and have neck plate communicators.

Birdman's enemies are more humanoid than those of Space Ghost. Many of the villains have pointy goatees: Reducto, Vulturo, the Chief of Fear, and Mentok, to name a few. University professors are also a part of the landscape with Birdman's friend Professor Demetrius or villains like Professor Nightshade. "Birdman" also had more action background music than "The Space Ghost."

During the 90s recycling, Birdman again followed in the footsteps of Space Ghost. Before embarking on his legal career in 2000, he was the substitute TV host for an AWOL Space Ghost in both "Pilot," 1997 and "Sequel," 1999.

Recontextualizing characters like Space Ghost, Brak, and Birdman is a wide open process left to one's imagination. Even after deciding on an office/workplace set, with antagonistic boss and employee relations like Space Ghost, Birdman could still be in any number of professions from a musician to a chef. Birdman wears appropriate attire for a lawyer in court, but, over his superhero costume with his mask and wings showing. Animated character costumes are basically the same for every episode, versus the live-action sitcom where they rarely wear the same clothes twice (independent of their character's economic status).

Birdman's new character, like Brak and Space Ghost, was modelled after shows from its originating era. "Perry Mason," 1957-66 set the standard for the TV lawyer/courtroom genre with 271 one hour episodes. Even iconic film directors got into the mix with Orson Welles' *The Trial* (1962), and "Alfred Hitchcock Presents: I Saw the Whole Thing," 1962. Space Ghost's profession is of 20th century origin whereas the legal profession is a few thousand years old; for example, Socrates (470-399 BC) opted against legal representation in his life or death trial.[1]

---

[1] Icarus, also Greek, is the opposite of Birdman-going nearer to the sun destroys him.

Birdman occasionally appears as a live-action character. In "Shaggy Busted" there is an in-episode promotion for the soft drink Tab at The Bird Cage bar; it turns into a live-action fantasy sequence with Birdman and a human size can of Tab on a date at the beach (Coke headquarters is in Atlanta). Further, in "Blackwatch Plaid" he is seen in several black-and-white surveillance cameras and he does a great long shot gag (characters are very small in the frame in relation to their surroundings) running back and forth, in jump cuts, across the front lawn of a mansion.

The show's 2005 promos had live-action characters, too, including a group of Orthodox Jews. Previously, any religious affiliation of Harvey Birdman had either been muted or nonexistent. Though not overtly clear in his name and profession change, it is suggested this superhero is an ethnic/religious stereo-type. Yet, I do not recall ever seeing or hearing any references to the Jewish faith in the cartoon: The Sabbath, synagogues, yarmulkes, etc. This was wise of the creators as people take most offense to religious humor. Protests, bans, legal action, and threats of violence are common responses.

Monty Python's *Life of Brian* (1979) UK was a period piece set in the time of Jesus Christ.[2] Its release was banned in Ireland, South Africa, Norway, and certain regions of its own country, England. There were also criminal blasphemy charges filed against the creators. Here in the United States there were complaints and protests about the film by Catholic, Lutheran, and Jewish organizations, but it did okay at the box office.

The 12 cartoons of Muhammad in the Danish newspaper Jyllands-Posten, 2/1/06, triggered worldwide protests, a United Nations complaint, and a failed attack on its newspaper building.[3] Sad to say, in 2015, twelve people were killed at The Charlie Hebdo magazine offices in Paris over a similar issue.[4]

The saga of "South Park" and religion is too long for this venue other than to note that a man who posted online threats to creators Trey Parker and Matt Stone was sentenced to 25 years in prison. Transferring their religious humor to the stage, the Broadway play *Book of Mormon* won nine Tony Awards in 2011 and broke many box office records.[5]

Even if "Harvey Birdman, Attorney at Law" did incorporate religious humor, that does not automatically make it offensive as each person has their own individual tolerance levels for each category of humor. Molly Shannon had an

---

[2] *Monty Python's Life of Brian Immaculate Edition, The Story of Brian,* Sony 2007. George Harrison of The Beatles provided most of the film's funding.

[3] http://www.msnbc.msn.com/id/11161015/displaymode/1107/s/2/ for the original cartoons; and msnbc.msn.com *Five held over 'imminent' terror attack on Danish cartoons newspaper,* Jan M. Olsen updated 12/29/10.

[4] *Charlie Hebdo Shootings: 12 Killed at Muhammad Cartoons Magazine in Paris*, NBC News, 1/7/15.

[5] edition.cnn.com *Man Who Threatened 'South Park' Creators Gets 25 Years In Prison,* Carol Cratty, 2/24/11; and tonyawards.com

SNL character, Mary Katherine Gallagher, that did soft Catholic religious humor. One of the tag lines from her film *Superstar* (1999) is " . . . a film of positive moral values . . . ." Yet, this is no guarantee that the entire film audience, nor the general public, felt that way. In the global media market there are normally multiple versions of an American product because it is edited to each nation's rules, including prevailing religious rules. Large segments of a film can be entirely omitted.[6] An SNL precedent of soft Catholic humor was the character Father Guido Sarducci (Don Novello). He provided a comic sermon at the Rally to Restore Sanity, National Mall, Washington DC, 10/30/10. Coorganizer Stephen Colbert, the March to Keep Fear Alive, voices the characters Reducto and Phil Ken Sebben on "Harvey Birdman, Attorney at Law," the latter a play on the character's original name in "Birdman," Falcon 7.

The other recycled Adult Swim shows limit themselves to a single 60s show for their cast. "Harvey Birdman, Attorney at Law" assembles its cast from multiple HB shows: Judge Mightor from "The Mighty Mightor"; Gigi from "The Galaxy Trio"; coworker Gleep from "The Herculoids"; and Potamus from "Peter Potamus and His Magic Flying Balloon." Though, the story line of each episode revolves around one particular Hanna-Barbera show, "Shaggy Busted" features "Scooby Doo," and "Back to the Future" features "The Jetsons," pause on a group shot and you can make out a list of all types of characters including current world leaders. Hanna-Barbera had earlier done the same for both TV shows and films; "Laff-a-Lympics," 1977 had three sports teams made up of characters from more than a dozen of its shows. This provided a sound business model for Adult Swim to build on.[7]

Cocreator Mike Ouweleen moved in-house from Adult Swim to Cartoon Network. This would not be uncommon for someone in comedy entertainment to work with media of different ratings. Historically, George Carlin (1937-2008) per his namesake website, played Mister Conductor in the G rated PBS children's show, "Shining Time Station," 1991-93 while previously he released "Class Clown: Seven Words You Can Never Say on Television," 1972. As is the case with stand-up comedians, over time there are multiple versions of the same routine, it morphed into "Filthy Words" at a 1982 Carnegie Hall performance. Ouweleen is currently the CMO of Cartoon Network, Adult Swim, and Boomerang.

---

[6] Will Ferrell (costar of *Superstar*) has two R rated versions of *Semi-Pro* (2008), in one Jackie Moon is married to a promiscuous spouse, in the other all scenes of her are omitted and he's single. Matt Walsh plays a Catholic priest/referee in it. Twenty years later Will and Molly are still working together as the comic news team Cord and Tish covering live events like the Rose Bowl Parade and The Royal Wedding.

[7] *The Art of Hanna-Barbera,* 1989, Hanna-Barbera/T. Sennett, 247-52, Viking Penguin. In 2002 Adult Swim aired an animated pilot of soft Jewish religious humor-"The Finkel Files."

"Sealab 2021," 2001-05.

"Frisky Dingo," 2006-08 (non-recycled).

Creators Adam Reed and Matt Thompson.

The original "Sealab 2020," 1972 (13 half hour episodes including three unaired) can be seen occasionally on sister station Boomerang. But unlike "The Space Ghost" and "Birdman" it has not been released on DVD.[1] It had a well balanced multicultural cast with two female aquanauts, one of whom was also a teacher. But there were still sexist undertones; at times Gail appeared weaker and almost childlike in relation to the male crew. The year "Sealab 2020" aired, 1972, was a would-be turning point in women's history as Congress passed the Equal Rights Amendment. For it to become law, though, thirty-eight states had to ratify it by 1979, which was then extended to 1982.

Amidst this hotbed of national debate, comedian Andy Kaufman (1949-84) began to wrestle women. As self proclaimed Intergender Champion from 1978-82, he wrestled at comedy clubs, arenas, and even on "Saturday Night Live." He would taunt his female opponents with lines like the following from the posthumous release *I'm From Hollywood* (1989): "I'm not saying women are mentally inferior to men because when it comes to things like, oh, cooking, cleaning, washing pots, scrubbing the carrots, raising the babies, mopping the floors, they have it all over men ... they're all oatmeal north of the eyebrows, they're all wheatina for brains ...." The payoff from these insults and the slapstick wrestling are the reaction shots of the incensed audience members, particularly the women.

Almost thirty years later, but only one year in the title story line, Gail of "Sealab 2020" has resurfaced as Debbie of "Sealab 2021" and she is far more of a sexist stereotype than her predecessor. It may have something to do with the fact that the Equal Rights Amendment for women NEVER became law (reaction shot on you the reader here) it needed a minimum of 38 states to ratify it, only 35 did!

"Sealab 2021" had a few episodes that may have broke comedy records at the time; for example, "Bizarro" with repetition and multiplication. The cast says the word "bizarro" over 100 times in 11 minutes. Bizarro Quinn is the worst offender, as he also repeats the phrases, "I'm helping" and "I love you."

---

[1] *Space Ghost & Dino Boy: The Complete Series;* and *Birdman & The Galaxy Trio: The Complete Series;* both Warner Bros. DVD, 2007.

Multiplication is seen in the bizarro duplicates. The creators later used this in the ad supported "Frisky Dingo: Pimp My Revenue," 2006: there are duplicate Stans; and "Scion" is said ten times and "Scion TC" 22 times in 11.5 minutes.

Borat, one of Sacha Baron Cohen's prank characters, has a great live-action repetition and multiplication counterpart on the DVD extras of *Borat: Cultural Learnings of America for Make Benefit Glorious Nation of Kazakhstan* (2007). First, a note on this film title, part of the joke was at the expense of the reviewers who needed to type out this long grammatically incorrect title in their articles. The press refused to do this for his subsequent film, and truncated its even longer title, *Bruno: Delicious Journeys Through America for the Purpose of Making Heterosexual Males Visibly Uncomfortable in the Presence of a Gay Foreigner in a Mesh T-Shirt* (2009), to *Bruno*.[2] In the four minute sixteen second *Supermarket,* foreigner Borat questions an American grocery store clerk about every single item on the top four shelves of a cheese case. While grasping or picking up each food item, he presents various configurations of the query word "This?"; such as "What is this?" "This is cheese?" "And this?" over 50 times. He then proceeds to the next two coolers (multiplication) using the same tactic 14 times with butter and finally twice with milk.His new prank series on Showtime "Who is America?" premieres tonight, 7/15/18.

Another likely record setting episode is "Fusebox," 2002 with its stalled establishing shot (the first shot following the titles). This exterior long shot of the underwater Sealab compound becomes a static long take lasting eight minutes, or eighty percent of the ten minute episode. No characters are visible through its darkened distant windows. The only visual action in the shot is an occasional school of fish crossing the frame horizontally, and some bubbles vertically. These fish are twice recycled as "Sealab 2020," 1972 borrowed them from the earlier HB underwater show "Moby Dick," 1967. To accentuate the visual inactivity there are also lengthy pauses in the dialogue. "Fusebox" is basically an inexpensive radio show, a successful throwback that demonstrates the underlying need for a strong audio track, especially in animation.

"Sealab 2020" was edited down from 21.5 minutes, not even airing a full season, to "Sealab 2021" 11 minutes that lasted four seasons. Following the recycled "Sealab 2021" was the new animation of both "Frisky Dingo" and the two episode special "The Xtacles," 2008, all from Seventy-Thirty Productions. Cocreator Adam Reed would go on to spend the following decade with his FX Network hit "Archer," 2009. The intro of "Archer: Riffs and Fugues," 2013 has Archer as Bob from "Bob's Burgers" (H. Jon Benjamin voices both characters).

---

[2] Sacha also used a lengthy title in his double book, *Borat: Touristic Guidings to Glorious Nation of Kazakhstan* and *Borat: Touristic Guidings to Minor Nation of U.S. and A.*, 2007. Sacha continues the repetition in the latter's text; read Borat's blow by blow description of a ping pong match, "Then I hit the ball to him, then he hit the ball to me, then I hit the ball to him, then he hit the ball to me, then I miss the ball." This is about 2% of the three pages, 87-89. The font size gets smaller and smaller as the match progresses.

Animation

"Aqua Teen Hunger Force," et al., 2001-15.
Creators Dave Willis and Matt Maiellaro.

Adult Swim's first in-house new (non-recycled) show debuted on 9/9/01, one week after the network's initial launch. Dave and Matt are both core Adult Swim personnel, their work dating back to "Space Ghost Coast to Coast," Matt from the first season. Both were involved with "Perfect Hair Forever," "Brak Presents the Brak Show Starring Brak," and a few "Sealab 2021" episodes such as "All That Jazz." Both have follow-up shows with Adult Swim: Dave has two current shows as cocreator of "Squidbillies" and the live-action "Your Pretty Face is Going to Hell"; and Matt's "12 oz. Mouse."

"Aqua Teen Hunger Force" (ATHF) made an attempt to premiere on "Space Ghost Coast to Coast" in 1999, but the script was never animated. So at the conclusion of the first season of ATHF in 2001, the original "Space Ghost Coast to Coast: Baffler Meal" script was animated, containing the readily apparent early design characters and voices.

Master Shake, Frylock, and Meatwad are based on a sound business tradition; America has a love affair with its snack and fast food mascots. Going back to, at least, 1916 Planters humanized a peanut and added some distinctive costume elements: a monocle, top hat, cane, gloves, and spats, creating Mr. Peanut. In 1954, two more iconic food items were humanized with the introduction of the M+M Spokescandies and the Kool-Aid Man.[1] To compliment these national brands, there are innumerable regional ones as well.

Aqua Teen Hunger Force Colon Movie Film For Theaters (2007) opens with classic 50s theater food mascots doing a song and dance routine from their era. A contemporary theater food mascot metal band appears, first scaring off the quartet and then threatening the film audience with "Cut You Up with a Linoleum Knife" (performed by Mastodon). One of the better film introductions ever!

The ad campaign for the film had a major glitch. Small magnetic light

---

[1] planters.com/history; kraftfoods.com/koolaid; and mms.com/usa. A singing group of claymation food mascots had a TV special "Meet the Raisins" and a TV series "California Raisins" in 1988; and a TV film *Raisins Sold Out: The California Raisins II* (1989).

sculptures of the Mooninite characters were placed in several cities across the country. On the morning of January 31, 2007, Boston Police and City officials believed these units were possibly improvised explosive devices. State, City, and Transit bomb squads were sent to multiple locations in the city. The Coast Guard and other regional Homeland Security staff assisted in shutting down parts of the city. The entire area went on high alert with televised broadcasts from both the Mayor and the Governor. I believe this event, and its subsequent fines, had some influence on the final cost of the film. Adult Swim bumps originally placed the cost of the film at a modest $750,000.00, but by 3/30/08 its bumps placed the cost at two million dollars.

Space Ghost (George Lowe) hosted a live webcast for its Atlanta film premiere. He interviewed several Adult Swim creators, while the crowd was able to meet Adult Swim costumed characters from both the film, and other AS shows including Stewie, Brian, Robot Chicken, Brak, and Harvey Birdman.

In response to the film's opening weekend reviews and gross, the stars of the film mounted a unique TV ad campaign. In one ad an agitated Carl spoke of 97 year old film reviewers, and about the audience, after having watched a really bad film instead of his, " . . . then go behind the theater and blow your face off with a shotgun. You're not good enough to see my ultra bad ass space movie . . .."

Adult Swim fans would be most familiar with gross-out humor through Tim and Eric's live-action antics. It is also the featured type of humor in this animated film. MC P Pants becomes a fly and snacks on a crusty white dog turd in the yard. Master Shake smashes him with a flyswatter, and then repeatedly hits Meatwad with the same now doubly gross item. The Mooninites ride a roller coaster and Ignignokt becomes ill. Err gives him a "thick shake" to drink to settle his stomach, but really, "It's mayonnaise I found in a trash can and it had hair on it!" Ignignokt twice pukes to Err's laughter. Carl, too, is having a nice dinner with Linda, and he inquires about his drink. When she replies that it is an, "Apple Cinnamon flavored monkey gland energy shake," he twice pukes on himself.

A live-action archetype film for gross-out humor is Linda Lautrec and Johnny Legend's *My Breakfast with Blassie* (1981) starring Andy Kaufman, a parody of Louis Malle's film *My Dinner with Andre* (1980). It is set in a restaurant and meant to resemble a real time, about an hour long, breakfast conversation between wrestler/comedian Andy Kaufman and wrestling icon Freddie Blassie.[2] The gross-out humor slowly amps up, from a normal sight of dunking toast in egg yolks to body hygiene discussions, such as fans wanting

---

[2] Freddie Blassie recorded a Johnny Legend song "Pencil Neck Geek" in 1974 and in 1977 it was #1 for 21 weeks on "The Dr. Demento Show" (per Fred Blassie on an undated video). Legend has an enviable skill set: musician, wrestler, wrestling manager, and filmmaker.

to shake their hands after going to the toilet, " . . . maybe their finger went right through the tissue"; to Andy's sale of used rubber snot.[3] Another diner (Bob Zmuda) visits their table twice, first pulling two bloody straws from his nose to give to Andy, and for the finale puking on Andy's dessert. The reaction shots from the gross-out humor are only in-part geared toward the older Freddie Blassie; the viewer is the main target, but there are no cameras on them.

The face of the vexed film ad campaign, the Mooninites, Ignignokt and Err, are ironically known for their pranks, especially prank phone calls to the Plutonians, Emery and Oglethorpe. It is an unusual subset of comedy that has its own history and rules. It has seen a resurgence with a puppet TV show based entirely around the concept "Crank Yankers," 2002-07, that featured many big comics like Jimmy Kimmel and Dave Chappelle. A recurring character on the show was Special Ed played by Jim Florentine of "That Metal Show." Don Jamison, also from the latter show, assists Jim on five volumes of "Terrorizing Telemarketers." In the U.K. it appears to be even bigger as Steve Penk has nine volumes of "Essential Windups." The English term is a good description as it attempts to wind up or rile up the phone prank victim. The G rated archetype for the prank phone call is "Jerry Lewis: Phoney Phone Calls 1959-1972," 2001. I have gleaned the following five prank call guidelines from this CD, and one track in particular, "Bill Lynch":

1) False identification (impersonation) is normally done by a prank phone caller, but the utmost in latitude is achieved when someone accidently calls a prankster. The unsuspecting caller (mis)dialed the number to the local pizza shop and thereby firmly believes that is who he or she is speaking with. The prankster can tell this caller almost anything.
2) Repeat back and verify incorrect information, purposely altering the facts (names, quantities, ingredients, times, addresses, etc.). Use repeatedly in the same call.
3) Varied speed of delivery-fast talking to drawn out; slowly confirm the spelling of a name, purposely mixing up one of its final letters. Use repeatedly in the same call.
4) Length of the call; how long can you can keep it going? The "Bill Lynch" track is 7.5 minutes but all of the business should normally be conducted in about a minute.
5) Victim's response level; how wound up or riled up can you get them (similar to a visual reaction shot)?

---

[3] Joe Pera was involved for years with The Andy Kaufman Award for comedy. His episode "Joe Pera Takes You to Breakfast," 2018 is an homage to Kaufman's only film, *My Breakfast with Blassie* (1981): arriving with a voice over to a real time breakfast restaurant shoot that includes geezers and extended talk of runny egg yolks; etc.

Many of these things can be illegal, so stick to analysis of recordings made by professional comedians. Has Bart Simpson been arrested for his prank calls to Moe's Bar?

The Plutonians add a different dynamic to the normal prank call as they demonstrate how not to do them. In "eDork," Oglethorpe fumbles his impersonation and the call lasts only 14 seconds. The Mooninites however, are adept at prank calls. In "Robositter" Err has a 40 second call to Oglethorpe that includes one false ID; two lewd name queries; two messages; and one strong response level-Oglethorpe throws a water balloon at his own monitor.

Hunter S. Thompson (1937-2005), famous American author and inventor of Gonzo Journalism, was renowned for telephoning people at all hours of the night.[4] His final article was written five days before his death on 2/15/05, *Shotgun Golf with Bill Murray* for ESPN.com Page 2; it includes the transcript of a 3:33 AM call to comedian Bill Murray of *Caddyshack* fame. In it Hunter explains a golf hybrid that uses a shotgun to take out the opponent's golf ball, "I see it as the first truly violent leisure sport."

Aqua Teen Hunger Force Zombie Ninja Pro-Am, 2007 for Playstation 2 is a golf game that includes Master Shake wielding a shotgun, along with a roof mounted bazooka on his golf cart. There are many Adult Swim games, some show based, for mobile, and PC and console. Scott Stoddard's *Robot Unicorn Attack* led the way and it has its own line of swag. There was an extensive line of ATHF swag, once including a $70,000.00 Meatwad Hot Air Balloon!

---

[4] An attempt at shotgun golf took place many years earlier, see *The Kitchen Readings,* 2008, pgs. 37-40. Bill Murray was the first actor to portray Hunter in *Where the Buffalo Roam* (1980). Murray's next film was *Caddyshack* (1980). Many attributes of Hunter's character are seen in Assistant Greenskeeper Carl Spackler: kind of shocking; an occasional grumbly, hard to understand voice; alcohol and marijuana props; and as an instigator of slapstick with multiple weapon props including a rake, a pitchfork (with Hunter's look-alike Dalai Lama in the dialogue), a fire extinguisher, a knife, a rifle, and explosives. The only other actor to portray Hunter was Johnny Depp in both *Fear and Loathing in Las Vegas* (1998) and *The Rum Diary* (2011).

"Squidbillies," 2005 to present.
Creators Dave Willis and Jim Fortier.

Early Cuyler premiered as a part of a film discussion panel in "Space Ghost Coast to Coast: Special Presentation," 2004. Early drank six fifths of xxx alcohol in about seven minutes and commenced to shoot Space Ghost, Zorak, Sharko, and Brak's Dad. Slapstick with a shotgun prop, normally keeping an unwanted away from them or off of their property, possibly a revenuer, a varmint, or a feuding neighbor, is part of a negative southern stereotype tradition. For some reason it flourished between 1962 and 1965. Along with Elvis' film *Kissin' Cousins* (1964) we see Hanna-Barbera (HB) start two new animated shows, "Punkin Puss," 1964 and "The Hillbilly Bears," 1965.

Even though there is a forty year gap, there are still many similarities between the HB cartoons and "Squidbillies." The lead male characters are all shoeless, wear grubby hats, and have barren wooden shacks with front porches. Early is taken a step further, being gap toothed like Cletus the slack jawed yokel from "The Simpsons." Common props of this genre include the following: corncob pipes, chew, a still and its product moonshine, rocking chairs, outhouses, whittling paraphernalia, farm animals, old trucks or hot rods, and bluegrass instruments. The Cuylers have updated this list with truck nuts and meth labs. Some of these "southern" props are also applicable to a general rural American negative stereotype. The accent, though, definitively attaches someone to a specific region.

Hanna-Barbera's first two TV series had southern accented lead characters both voiced by Daws Butler: Reddy from "The Ruff and Reddy Show," 1957; and Huckleberry Hound from his self-titled 1958 show. Neither of these characters nor Drooper of HB's "Banana Splits" exhibit any of the aforementioned negative stereotypes. There is Luke and Blubber's still powered Arkansas Chuga-bug in "The Wacky Races," 1968, but another non negative southerner from this show gets her own spin-off, "The Perils of Penelope Pitstop," 1969.

The archetype of the negative southern stereotype comes from the earlier, "Sealab 2021," referenced *Andy Kaufman: I'm From Hollywood* (1989). Being Intergender Champion was only a part of Andy Kaufman's antagonistic wrestling character. He chose to wrestle out of Memphis, Tennessee, in part for the music parody it provided, as it was home to Elvis Presley, aka The King. Southern Wrestling Champion Jerry Lawler later adopted the moniker "King" wearing a crown and royal cape, and holding a sceptre. This was Andy's wrestling nemesis, so Andy performed an original song and dance for Jerry and the arena crowd, "I'm the King of Tennessee." It ends with some juvenile mimicry baiting, that when executed properly can elicit a response from even the most reserved adult.

He would further insult the regional southern wrestling audience about their purported ignorance, poverty, and hygiene deficiencies, recommending soap, toilet paper, and razors for the women-an added sexist layer. His wrestling character uses his real name and position as the famous and wealthy TV actor that plays Latka in "Taxi," 1978-82. He uses his real manager, George Shapiro, as a wrestling manager and pits his adopted hometown of Hollywood against Memphis. So there are multiple layers to his comedy: sexist, socioeconomic, anti-southern regional, music parody, costume, juvenile humor, and the history of professional wrestling featuring slapstick.

"Squidbillies" cast member Granny (a drag voice by Dana Snyder, who did Master Shake) provides the geezer humor; it is a stock southern stereotype character, the most notorious being Granny of "The Beverly Hillbillies," 1962-71. Old folks and their aging issues make for an easy comic target: deterioration of mental and physical health; lack of independence and finances; keeping up to date with technology and trends; and their challenged love life. The latter issue also includes geezers making romantic advances toward much younger people. This is a standard with both Mel Brooks, Bialystock has to sleep with many little old lady investors in *The Producers* (1967) and (2005); and several of Adam Sandler's Happy Madison films, for example, *Grandma's Boy* (2006). The latter becomes a double entendre title as the story line amorously pairs Nick Swardson's young adult character, Jeff, with Shirley Jones' promiscuous grandma character, Grace.

The animated Granny in "Squidbillies" is worse, referencing interspecies sex, incest, and suggested pedophilia in, for example, "Clowny Freaks," 2010 with Granny attempting to solicit sex from underage boys at a birthday party.

The setting for the show is 109 miles north of Atlanta, so it is only fitting that an Atlanta company, Radical Axis, does the animation for this, and other Adult Swim shows (both show creators are from North Georgia, too). The Sheriff is a unique character with two different size arms, his right being half as thick as his left, and a distinct walk cycle that is more of a sideway shuffle.[1]

"Squidbillies" holds the record for longevity in southern stereotype TV comedies surpassing all three 60s shows, two HB cartoons and the live-action "The Beverly Hillbillies." Adult Swim has spread the regional humor locales into animated pilots "The Southies" for Boston and "Chuck Deuce" for Santa Cruz; and the live-action season 1 hit "Joe Pera Talks With You" for Michigan.

---

[1] Predecessor Sheriff Alabama oversees an amalgamated south in 70s underground comic *E.Z. Wolf* by Ted Richards. The cover for *WWE Heroes #0* prequel comic, 2010 is drawn by Jerry "The King" Lawler.

"12 oz. Mouse," 2005-06.

Creator Matt Maiellaro.

The following series of bumps were played just prior to its premiere: "... The Story of 12 oz. Mouse: ... Animated on a card table. With a #2 pencil. By M. Maiellaro....." The simple character designs and the sparse sets have an impressive lineage. Mouse is similar in design to Ignatz mouse of "Krazy Kat," 1962 as both have a bright single color body, head, and ears, with black stick-figure legs, arms, and tail. Both are criminals and have cops for costars.[1]

Rural Ignatz had an exotic colorful desert in contrast to the sparse urban one of Mouse. A precursor set was in the early 60s "Tooter Turtle." Depending on the episode, much if not all of the set (including the ground, buildings, trees, and sky) is monochromatic, a single tan or ivory color, and it can have a few select small or large items that are in color. The signature Tooter Turtle space spin is also seen with Mouse in "Bowtime."

Mouse's supporting cast is unusual. Rhoda the bartender (voiced by Dave Willis) was created from a piece of paper torn from a "Perfect Hair Forever" script; you can read some of the dialogue along with the names of two of its characters, Coiffio and Cat Man, who are also voiced by Dave. The barely mobile and now talking Shark is recycled from "Space Ghost Coast to Coast: Kentucky Nightmare," 2001. Sidekick Skillet has no English dialogue; he just squeals. Skillet was involved in, I believe, a record breaking television performance in "Spider, Version 2." He played a 3.5 minute drum solo, comprising almost one third of the entire episode length. Mouse, the guitarist of this musical duo, provides a venue for creator Matt's guitar skills.

Matt's formal film training shines through with his variety of compound shots. "Rememorized" has a 3.5 minute single camera long take/deep focus shot. Mouse and Skillet are in a lengthy gun battle (add shot count here) in the street in the deep; the cop is inside the diner in the foreground unaware of them; and in the midground is the diner's front window that includes an alternate focal point of a flashing and buzzing red neon sign. The camera track/zooms on occasion with an accompanying eerie audio effect. The lyrics of Def Leppard's "Foolin" are layered into the beginning of the cop's soliloquy. "12 oz. Mouse" was one of the few shows on Adult Swim that used advanced layering of visual and audio film techniques. A brand new clip was shown on "Development Meeting," 6/24/18...

[1] "Krazy Kat" can be traced back to the original Keystone Kops with K. K. initials as its long running newspaper comic strip and film shorts, 1909-44, began about the same time as Keystone, 1912.

"The Jellies," 2017 to present.
Creators Tyler Okonma and Lionel Boyce.

We are in the third week of Tyler, The Creator's (Tyler Okonma) new animated show on Adult Swim "The Jellies." Cocreated with fellow Odd Future member and "Loiter Squad" alumnus, Lionel Boyce, and animated by Brooklyn's Augenblick Studios ("Superjail!").

Cartoon Network and Adult Swim executives had earlier launched another great music artist into animation with André Benjamin's (André 3000 of Outkast) "Class of 3000," 2006. An excellent show set in Atlanta and geared toward a younger audience. André was 31 at his launch whereas Tyler is only 26 for "The Jellies." Note, in between these two shows, in 2010, Adult Swim did a TV special "Freaknik: The Musical" that likely holds the all time record for the largest group of popular music artists in an animated work with T-Pain, Snoop Dogg, Lil Wayne, and many more, see "The Brak Show" and "Cartoonography."

Tyler's earlier live-action work for Adult Swim, "Loiter Squad," was produced by Dickhouse of "Jackass" and included some of its characteristic physical stunts and pranks, along with in-episode and live performance music. Tyler has a new live-action show, too, on Viceland, "Nuts + Bolts." Tyler, along with cohost Davon Jasper Wilson, Odd Future member and "Loiter Squad" alumnus, creates his own products based on that episode's guests. "Breakfast" for example, has him visit Crown Maple Syrup farm in the Hudson Valley, where he creates his own flavor Cinnamint maple syrup. The product is available in limited supply at Crown Maple and soon to be on Tyler's website golfwang.com adding to his current array of Golf items.[1] Other "Nuts + Bolts" episodes include bedroom furniture, Converse sneakers, and even a go-kart.[2] He is building an empire of items that we need to keep an eye out for at both national retailers and the brand new Golf Wang store in Los Angeles.

At San Diego Comic Con in 2017 Tyler responds to an audience question about "The Jellies," "[H]ow many f$#ckin black cartoon characters is it on TV

---

[1] One of Tyler's "Loiter Squad" characters, Thurnis Haley, is a golfer and sometimes, I believe, he wears a Golf brand button up shirt.

[2] The first episode of "Nuts and Bolts" includes a Tyler original stop-motion short made at Stoopid Buddy Studios of "Robot Chicken" fame. So, Tyler has worked in multiple formats: animation, both 2D and stop-motion, live-action, and recorded and performance music. We'll wait and see if there are Tyler games, live streams, books, or films to follow.

right now? Name five, I'll give you time. [I]t is none! [H]e aint got no guns, he aint shooting no f$#ckin basketball, and he a f$#ckin goober…[a]nd he's the lead character."

"The Jellies" are a suburban family of jellyfish with one human 16 year old son, Cornell Jelly. Story lines revolve around family life with a twist. In "Ray's Perfect Date" there is a Tyler song about Jamelah set to a black-and-white urban montage, a great contrast to the wonderful color of the series. Along with the latter constant, there are brief scenes that include other Augenblick traits such as multiple character super violence (in some "Superjail!" scenes there are too many violent acts to count at regular speed). "Ray's Perfect Date" is a parody of reality TV including "True Life," "Catfish," "16 and Pregnant," and "Pimp My Ride." A military unit attempts to attack Xzibit on a reality show set and over a 20 second period instead decimates all of the film crews. To add to the multiple characters there are multiple clones of Xzibit in three scenes. The predecessor "The Boondocks: The Real" is another reality TV parody that featured Xzibit, and "Extreme Makeover: Home Edition." To date Tyler and Lionel write-in a lot of throwback music artists. "The Jellies: Gangsta's Paradise" and the live-action "Black Jesus: Gangsta's Paradise" feature Coolio and are titled after his 1995 song. "The Jellies" premiere of this episode on 10/23/17 was preceded by "Squidbillies: The Guzzle Pumpkin" that also included a cameo of Coolio.

Both "Superjail!" in animation, and "Loiter Squad" in live-action, used gross out humor. For example, in "Ray's Perfect Date" Jamelah, wearing a blood soaked nightshirt, vomits green four times.

It will be fun to watch the rest of the premiere season and to monitor the growth of Tyler's Bald Fade Productions. Its live-action logo is a point-of-view shot from Tyler pushing a person who drops a hot dog on the ground accompanied by the dialogue "Hey hemi, that's my hot dig."

Tyler TV has "Loiter Squad" and two shows on two networks, "Nuts + Bolts" and "The Jellies." Tyler, The Creator is currently on the Flower Boy music tour.

"Lucy, The Daughter of the Devil," 2007.
Creator Loren Bouchard.

The creator and most of the voice cast are from "Home Movies": Melissa Galsky as both Lucy and Becky; H. Jon Benjamin as Special Father Giuseppe Cantalupi and Lucy's Dad, Satan (with two different size eyes like his second character, Jason, from "Home Movies"); and Eugene Mirman doing a drag voice for Special Sister Mary.

"Lucy, The Daughter of the Devil" is a mix of the horror genre and Catholic religious humor; the regular cast includes Jesus, two priests, a nun, an alter boy, and in the episode below a visit from the Pope. It is still the only new Adult Swim series titled after a female! The Japanese reclamation "Super Milk Chan," 2004 was titled after its young female star, but it did not air that long on Adult Swim. A more recent Toonami show "Pop Team Epic," 2018 stars the teenage female comedy team of Popuko and Pipimi.

Like the concurrent anime parody "Perfect Hair Forever," LTDOTD had a different title and credit sequence for every episode. The credits for the series finale "Monster" had an over two minute phone conversation between Lucy and her Dad, where she pranks him into thinking that she is pregnant. This high quality lengthy audio interaction is a carryover from "Home Movies."

Fluid Animation added a CG twist and placed the set of the show in its hometown of San Francisco. The Golden Gate Bridge scene in "Monster" was a parody of *It Came from Beneath the Sea* (1955); a sci-fi thriller that had a giant octopus attack San Francisco (Ray Harryhausen did the FX, read more about his work in "Robot Chicken"). The musical element of "Home Movies" is carried over with DJ Jesus (Jon Glaser of "Delocated" and "Neon Joe, Werewolf Hunter") here beatboxing the giant monster from a helicopter. Lucy destroys the monster with mace, an entry/exit, as she maced him through the phone in the prologue.

A film blueprint would be *Little Nicky* (2000), Satan as Dad with the child's name as the title. Further Satan based Adult Swim comedies would include "Mr. Pickles" and the live-action "Your Pretty Face is Going to Hell."

"Home Movies: Camp," 2004, the premiere episode of its final season, was a precursor to the character Lucy, and "Metalocalypse": Melissa was dressed as Satan with devil horns and introduced a "devil music" band that performed "Welcome To Hell."

"Metalocalypse," 2006-13.

Creators Brendon Small and Tommy Blacha.

Brendon's second character in "Home Movies," Duane, was the singer and lead guitarist of the aforementioned "devil music" band. He had long hair and wore a charcoal outfit with a jawless skull emblem on his chest. Skwisgaar Skwigelf of "Metalocalypse" became his Swedish reincarnation: a long haired lead guitarist that wears a charcoal outfit with a jawless skull belt buckle. Duane was animated with only four fingers and a guitar with no strings, whereas Skwisgaar has all five fingers and a fully detailed Gibson.

Brendon is the voice actor for two other Dethklok band members: lead singer Nathan Explosion; and drummer Pickles with a Wisconsin regional accent. Cocreator Tommy does the remaining two voices of the band: bassist William Murderface; and Norwegian guitarist Toki Wartooth. The twos Northern Europeans bands members whats plays guitars (what began as a typo demonstrates their accents and excessive use of plurals due to a limited knowledge of the English language) provide great national humor. The Finnish Dudesons are a forerunner to both the American Jackass troupe and Dethklok's extreme cartoon slapstick. They have an enormous catalogue of stunts, such as Demolition Man, but one series, Mr. Hitler has a personal backstory-revenge pranks on their bully adult neighbor from childhood: excavating and camouflaging a hole in his driveway that would fit his entire car; defecating in his mailbox; and blasting him with a waste cannon from a tanker truck. Unlike Toki and Skwisgaar, Jarppi, Jukka, Jarno, and HP have excellent English language skills, so it was just Finnish names, accents, and sets with live-action cartoon violence. *The Dudesons Prank Book,* 2011, Finland, is illustrated like a cartoon storyboard.

Brendon did a little work for PETA and this influence is seen in the themes of "Dethfashion" and "Fatklok." For the latter the band adopts a human teenage son for tax reasons and names him Fatty Ding Dong. Meeting the fate of some unfortunate adopted dogs there is both neglect-left on a short chain alone outdoors with no shelter and little, no, or poor food and water; physical abuse-tasered in the veterinarian's waiting room (where we also see a dog portrait on the wall that resembles Brendon's dog Ernie); and abandonment-"setting him free" in the country to disaster, mauled by cats, a classic "Metalocalypse" ending of gore and mayhem. Dethklok came up with this release plan after Fatty accidentally killed The London Philharmonic with lasers.

Comic books are a perfect fit for extreme slapstick. Dark Horse did a one-shot *Dethklok Versus The Goon* in 2009. It worked so well, it gave the band their own comic and it ran for two more issues. All are available in a compilation hardcover.

"Metalocalypse" began as a 15 minute show but was extended to a half hour due to its popularity. Gibson created a high end guitar in its name, an almost unprecedented sign of the popularity of an animated TV band. The Dethklok Thunderhorse Explorer was released in 2011 and retailed from $1,670 to $2,799. "Thunderhorse" is a music video from its second episode "Dethwater," 2006. Gibson had plans for a Toki style guitar and a Murderface bass, too.

Brendon headed a live version of the Dethklok touring band that regularly sold out its venues. It was a quartet, not a quintet, as Brendon simultaneously handled the roles of the singer and lead guitarist from the cartoon band.

Titmouse has produced or coproduced a multitude of other Adult Swim shows and specials, too: "China, IL," 2008-15; "Freaknik: The Musical," 2010; "Black Dynamite," 2011; "The Venture Bros." and "Superjail!," 2011 forward; "Brad Neely's Harg Nallin' Sclopio Peepio," 2016; and "Ballmastrz 9009," 2018.

Dethklok had a live band, five audio CDs (see "The Brak Show"), three comic books, a high end guitar replica, and two Guitar Hero releases, *Thunderhorse* and *Laser Cannon Deth Sentence*. The TV show spread into multiple formats, a sure sign of success. At one point, you could even purchase a Dethklok fountain at adultswim.com for $40,000.00! I inquired by telephone and it appeared to be a real company with detailed construction plans. I don't know if there were ever any takers.

Brendon has moved on to *Galaktikon* comics, audio CDs, and a recent live-action short film *Galaktikon: Nightmare* (2018) for Funny or Die. He has plans to add a game in the near future. Tommy continued with the animated slapstick in "Mongo Wrestling Alliance."

"Mongo Wrestling Alliance," 2011.
Creator Tommy Blacha.

Tommy worked as a Creative Director for WWE in 1999, so coupled with his "Metalocalypse" animation background, he had the perfect qualifications for this show. "Mongo Wrestling Alliance" was somewhat of a new venture in TV animation as "Mucha Lucha!" 2002-05 was a family comedy, and "Hulk Hogan's Rock 'N' Wrestling," 1985-87 used animated versions of real life professional wrestlers. For the latter, there was an established name recognition. It's taking a while for me to become personally involved with this large cast of characters; the star's name, Rusty Kleberkuh, has finally sunk in. This is the landscape of a new TV show, establishing an environment along with character name recall. Creating funny names for new characters, and here also wrestling holds, is a big part of comedy. The star's name is said in the following ways during "Presumed Imbecile": Rusty, eight times; Rusty Kleberkuh, four times; Mr. Kleberkuh once (and not counting "stupid" once); and it is chanted seven times for a total of 20 times in 10.5 minutes, minus the title and credits.

Per an interview with Tommy on the Edge and Christian's podcast, he's working on a book now about wrestling and early TV. Yes, if you're interested in comedy, study vintage wrestling footage for characters/costumes, story lines, audience interaction, interviews, and slapstick. The early regional TV broadcasts are great but many of my favs are still only sold in the VHS format; national broadcasts took over in the mid 70s. Read about early 80s wrestling with Andy Kaufman in "Sealab 2021," "Aqua Teen Hunger Force," "Squidbillies," and Color Art.

Seth Green and Stoopid Buddy Stoodios have created two wrestling shows since the cancellation of "Mongo Wrestling Alliance." In 2014 they made 26 episodes of the stop-motion short "WWE Slam City." In 2016 and 2018 they made two seasons, five episodes each, of the 2D "Camp WWE." This show is groundbreaking in that several actual wrestlers do their own voices, excluding child versions, so "Camp WWE" has addressed the issues of the preceding animated wrestling shows. Seth Green was host of "Monday Night Raw" in 2009 and wrestled in a six man tag team match with Triple H and John Cena versus Randy Orton and The Legacy. His costume featured a Stoopid Monkey tee-shirt. An animated wrestling show appears to be a tough genre to sustain, but what fun!

"Rick and Morty," 2013 to present.
Creators Dan Harmon and Justin Roiland.

The season 3 finale gave Adult Swim its highest ratings ever. In fact, "Rick and Morty" was the number one comedy in America for millennials.[1] The Rickmobile has toured the US for the past two years from May through October. "Rick and Morty" appears to be on track (70 more episodes) to have the deepest line of merchandise ever for a TV show: from standard items of apparel, action figures, and plush toys to the following food and beverages: Exploding Meeseeks Blue Razz Bar, Pickle Flavored Dark Chocolate, Squanchin' Creamsicle Bar, Pickle Rick Pickle In A Pouch, Rick's Love Potion Energy Shot, Fleeb Juice Energy Drink, Pickle Rick Soda, and Strawberry Smiggles Cereal.

So, what happened on 10/7/17 with the limited relaunch of McDonald's *Mulan* Szechuan McNugget Sauce from '98? McDonald's had a Disney Happy Meal since '87, so it had a 20 year history of film promotions. These films, though, were all for children, G or PG rated. In 2005, McDonald's used in-film advertising with *The Longest Yard,* a PG-13 film costarring Terry Crews as Cheeseburger Eddy, a prison inmate.[2] "Rick and Morty" had the next rating, "Adult" Swim, a new demographic where McDonald's shockingly underestimated the demand. Police were called in several US cities for crowd control at its release. McDonald's then created a three installment podcast of *The Sauce* addressing the debacle; and four months later it released 20 million packets.[3]

"Rick and Morty: State of Georgia vs. Denver Fenton Allen," 2016 is a 9.5 minute super low budget short. There is one black-and-white with gray illustration of Judge Morty, and one of defendant Rick with his lawyer; the two stars have adjusting facial expressions and an occasional head nod, the rest is all camera placement and editing. There are two more illustrations, the court reporter (speaks only two words) and the court officer, both used for reaction shots. It is a word for word actual trial transcript, so no new script, with Justin Roiland doing both voices. There is a lot of repetition, as in the show but without the added multiples of Rick and Morty or others, using curse words and sexual humor. An example of what can be done with just a storyboard.

[1] *Animation Magazine: 'Rick and Morty' Breaks Ratings Records,* 10/4/17. Cameron Koller.

[2] We had a Cheeseburger Eddy Day on 3/31/15 in the Adam Sandler course. Terry Crews was super nice and called in with a few voice messages for the class giving us some backstory on *The Longest Yard*, with cheeseburgers and Quarter Pounders for all. The Szechuan Sauce rant is in "The Rickshank Rickdemption," its title from another prison film.

[3] *Toppodcast.com: The Sauce – McDonald's/Studio@ Gizmodo/Onion Labs* (n.d.). *Eater, LA: Police Called in to Control Rick and Morty Szechuan Sauce Fiasco at La Brea McDonald's,* 10/9/17, Mona Holmes.

"The Venture Bros.," 2004 to present.

Creator Christopher McCulloch, aka Jackson Publick.

"The Venture Bros." is the longest running new half hour show on Adult Swim. Part of its recipe for success is a large and varied cast. It included 70s music icons Iggy Pop and David Bowie, too, though not voiced by the actual people, as recurring characters. Their dialogue often included their song titles and lyrics. Other characters were also named from their lyrics such as with David Bowie's Major Tom from "Space Oddity," 1969, and Action Man from "Ashes to Ashes," 1980; and both characters speak in lyrics from their host and other Bowie songs, "TVC 15," 1976 dominates their opening dialogue in "Ghosts of the Sargasso." Bowie's "Scary Monsters (And Super Creeps)," 1980 was the background song for some of the show's 2018 promos. A similar technique is common in wind ups, aka prank calls, made popular by English comic Steve Penk-see how many song titles and lyrics of a certain recording artist you can include in one telephone conversation; he has a "David Bowie Song Titles" cut on "Essential Windups Volume 4."[1]

Keeping with the classic rock theme Christopher McCulloch created a character based on legendary *Rolling Stone* writer Dr. Hunter S. Thompson (1937-2005) naming him Colonel Hunter Gathers (I was tempted to put the middle initial "S." in there). The Colonel, now General, is very similar in voice (mumbling to yell), appearance (including the props of aviator sunglasses, cigarette in holder, a pistol in a shoulder or side holster, a knife, and a hat-but not his signature boonie style), and action (in "Assissinanny 911," for example, he throws a grenade into a pool with compressed air tanks nearby). In the same episode Colonel Hunter says to Brock, "Can you keep your head about you when confronted with mindblowing weirdness at every turn?" which refers back to famous Hunter S. Thompson quotes, "It never got weird enough for me," or "When the going gets weird, the weird turn professional." Even the sets are accurate, in "Orb," 2008, he is employed at a gentleman's club and Hunter S. Thompson was, for story research in 1985, the night manager of the O'Farrell Theatre gentleman's club in San Francisco. In a few episodes Colonel Hunter is transgender: he appears in drag in "Orb" as a female Parisian sniper; and in "Assissinanny 911," 2006 as a transsexual on the operating table in the midst of, at least, a breast implantation. Hunter S. Thompson occasionally appeared in partial drag, with lipstick and a hat that

---

[1] A tribute bar called Ziggy's opened 9/18 in London and the cocktails are named from the CD's song titles and lyrics.

resembles a blonde wig with long pigtails per *Breakfast with Hunter* (2003).

Ralph Steadman is the artist that illustrated most all of Hunter's writings, and in his posthumous tribute book *The Joke's Over*, 2006 (also see his *Gonzo The Art,* 1998) he includes a few portraits of a transsexual Hunter: a nude of Hunter's top half with female breasts (page 353); and a full figure illustration of Hunter standing in red high heels with red finger nails in the desert, and a collage of a woman placed inside the top half of his body frame (page 342).[2] For the latter, *Doomed Love at the Taco Stand, Hunter S. Thompson,* 1997 Ralph explains "It is a picture of him as a 15 year old nymphette trapped inside the body of a 60 year old drug fiend." A further element of the drag comedy here is that Hunter had an imposing 6'6" frame. See two Hunter S. Thompson portraits by Ralph Steadman in Color Art.[3]

Colonel Hunter Gathers was not the first cartoon characterization of Hunter S. Thompson. Pulitzer Prize winning newspaper comic strip *Doonesbury,* 1970 by Gary Trudeau included the character Uncle Duke, named after Hunter's quasi autobiographical character Raoul Duke from *Fear and Loathing in Las Vegas,* 1971. Trudeau later created a CG/puppet version of Uncle Duke to be used in a run for U.S. President in 2000; the campaign launch was in Aspen, Hunter's hometown. The Uncle Duke puppet further did remotes on the talk show circuit with "Larry King Live" and "The Today Show." Hunter S. Thompson states, "If you want to be a famous American writer, you don't really think of being in the comic strips." Pat Caddell further paraphrases Hunter, "He hated *Doonesbury,* he hated being a caricature . . . it interfered with him being a reporter."[4] The more innovative Colonel Hunter Gathers of "The Venture Bros." was created posthumously as an homage.

Christopher McCulloch, the creator, does several of the voices, in particular, General Hunter. Doc Hammer, artist, musician (the band Weep), cowriter, editor, and voice actor also assists. This was a brief two character study, if you were to do the entire cast of "The Venture Bros." it would be a very long piece. Their new book, *Go Team Venture!: The Art and Making of The Venture Bros.,* 2018, is 376 pages. There is always great swag for this show from the tee shirts at Astro Base Go to odd items advertised during breaks: sheets; and a call-in, using a character voice, for a chance to buy a limited edition ice cream cake!

---

[2] *Ralph Steadman: A Retrospective* is currently on display at American University. Some D.C. Metrobuses are covered in giant wraps of his work. There is a great documentary film on Ralph, *For No Good Reason* (2012) UK.

[3] The first time Ralph worked with Hunter, *The Kentucky Derby is Decadent and Depraved,* 1970 Scanlan's Monthly, he had to do on the spot drawings with only an eyebrow pencil and lipstick.

[4] doonesbury.com. Uncle Duke is likely a big part of the back story for Hunter's tirade about cartoons in *Breakfast with Hunter* (2003), Wayne Ewing. All of the quotes are from *Gonzo: The Life and Work of Dr. Hunter S. Thompson* (2008), Alex Gibney; and Ralph Steadman's quote is from *Special Features*. Also from the latter, Ralph performs, in drag, a comic parody of the Eric Idle song "Bright Side of Life" from *Monty Python's Life of Brian* (1979) UK. He is wearing a women's white Kentucky Derby hat with netting, atop a messy blonde wig, with extreme red lipstick, and dark sequins. A well armed English dame holding a pistol in his right hand, and later Hunter gives him a stun gun for his left.

"Tom Goes to the Mayor," 2004-06.

Creators Tim Heidecker and Eric Wareheim.

An innovative and economical animation process using approximately one thousand altered still photos per episode that required no lip synch, launched Tim and Eric's career at Adult Swim. They had many shorts from college and beyond, see the TIMANDERIC.COM DVD, and most were live-action, but the four minute *Tom Goes To The Mayor* (2001-02) was the one AS wanted first.

In the original short Tom is a restauranteur, trying to sell the Mayor on a pair of new restaurants, Skooners and Gullivers. Tom draws a childlike sketch of the buildings and food items and recites a few of the seafood dishes, " . . . trout, fried fillet of trout, trout borghese, and trout fries."

In their second short film *Tom Goes To The Mayor Returns* (2003) they are going over plans for the Lobster Day parade. The Mayor recites the following nine dishes, "baked lobster, broiled lobster roll, twice baked lobster tail, lobster dumplings, breaded lobster, stuffed lobster, lobster bisque, lobster chowder, and lobster salad." A predecessor for their food lists is in *Cracking Up* (1983). A waitress (Zane Buzby) gives Jerry Lewis exactly one hundred food and drink choices in three minutes, including 18 different salad dressings, "vinegar, vinegar and oil, plain oil, thousand island, hundred island, hawaiian island, three mile island, russian, german, swiss, mayo, roquefort, blue cheese, brown cheese, cheese, cheese and bacon, bacon bits, bacon chips."

A giant robotic lobster claw and a 200 gallon pot of boiling butter are proposed floats for the Lobster Day parade. These giant items carry over into the TV series, too, for example, the giant eclair in "WW Laserz." Mitch Hedberg, the king of food jokes, has a similar surreal line with, "I want to make a vending machine that sells vending machines, it'd have to be real f##$ing big." Almost one third of the material on Mitch's three audio CDs is food related. I will give a few examples yet so many to choose from, the possessive of Reese's, anchovies, Sprite recipe, Benihana to go, cake eaters, and so forth: "I had a piece of Care Free sugarless gum, and I was still worried, it never kicked in! I took it back to the store and said 'Bullsh*t.'"; or " . . . I don't need a receipt for the donut, man, I'll just give you the money then you give me the donut, end of transaction, we don't need to bring ink and paper into this, I just can't imagine a scenario where I'd have to prove I bought a donut." Mitch's only film *Los Enchiladas!* (1999) is set in a restaurant.

Gullivers Old (New) World Buffet became a main set in the series "Tom Goes To The Mayor." The title sequence is almost entirely Gullivers related, from Gullivers' snow globes to the City Council meetings that regularly take place there.[1] Tim and Eric feature the more gross-out elements of food comedy. In "Friendship Alliance" Tom and John (John C. Reilly) go to Sauceman's where you bring your own meat and there are over 1,000 dipping sauces, they demonstrate this with live-action shots of gooey hands full of meat dipping in all of the sauce bowls. In "Vice Mayor" Tom has three big plates of cheese flavored fries at Turners and there is a composite shot close-up of his mouth full of them. There are multiple other examples including "Puddins," "My Big Cups," and General Patton's Grille in "WW Laserz."

Food is a common prop in comedy and it is trending this decade. Comedian Gabriel Iglesias has a cake as his moniker and fans bring countless cakes to him at his performances. Jim Gaffigan is associated with Hot Pockets. Tim and Eric's Abso lutley Productions works on "The Eric Andre Show." Eric has several skits with ranch dressing, and, in 2016, he had a ranch pop-up shop in NYC with a ranch fountain, swag, and drinking contests. Though not comedies, there are a lot of food contest and travel shows. Eric was a guest judge on "Knife Fight: Collins vs. Feau" on Food Network in 2013. Tim and Eric had at least one guest comic for every episode of TGTTM, some for lunch or dinner, and this prepped them for a return to their live-action roots with characters like Spagett in "Tim and Eric Awesome Show, Great Job!" and Gary the sauce boy in "Tim and Eric's Bedtime Stories."

[1] Carrying on the political theme of TGTTM, both Eric Andre and Tim Heidecker did separate on the street shoots at The Republican National Convention in Cleveland. Tim released a music CD "Too Dumb For Suicide: Tim Heidecker's Trump Songs," in 2017 and campaigned for District Attorney of San Bernardino County in 2018. His character Decker works at The White House.

Live-Action

"Tim and Eric Awesome Show, Great Job!," 2007-10.
"Tim and Eric's Bedtime Stories," 2013 to present.
Creators Tim Heidecker and Eric Wareheim.
"On Cinema," 2012 to present, and "Decker," 2014 to present.
Creators Tim Heidecker and Gregg Turkington.

In July, 2011 Tim and Eric Awesome Tour, Great Job played at the Iveagh Gardens comedy festival in Ireland (with rave reviews) and to sold out shows in London theatres. In 2017, Tim and Neil Hamburger (Gregg Turkington) performed at the Soho in London. A one-off "Tropical Cop Tales" premiered on Adult Swim 7/30/18, a product of English director/writer Jim Hosking that featured geezer and gross out humor. Adult Swim had earlier reclaimed a few Britcoms with only limited success: "Look Around You," 2002-05, UK; "Garth Marenghi's Darkplace," 2004, UK; and "The Mighty Boosh," 2003-07, UK. The latter was the most successful, yet, I'm surprised it was not a big hit. Noel Fielding and Julian Barratt were an awesome comedy team that, like Tim and Eric, created fun music with imaginative characters and costumes, such as Old Gregg and Milky Joe, and worked in both animation and live-action.

Adult Swim did not go into live-action until five and a half years after its launch, it is "Cartoon" Network after all. The first showing was a double bill of 15 minute shows on 2/12/07 with "Tim and Eric Awesome Show, Great Job!: Dads" and "Saul of the Mole Men: A New Friend." The latter was an excellent series with costumes and puppets but short lived. "Fat Guy Stuck In Internet: Threshold" premiered three months later on 5/13/07 and met the same fate.

One element that most reviewers would think is a major drawback is that much of their troupe of recurring actor/comedians is hardly well known: ventriloquist Dave Liebe Hart; comic James Quall; actor/singer Ron Austar; and actress Carol Kraft. The latter appears as Carol with Zach Galifianakis in "Greene Machine," but not on her usual set as Carol Krabit of Channel 5 News' "Yesterdays Weather." Their lesser known cast members mix well with the big name guest comics, though, at some point everyone in the entertainment field is lesser known.

The Three Stooges are a major influence when Zach G. and Tim and Eric work together. "Bedtime Stories: Bathroom Boys," 2014 has the trio with distinctive hair styles-Zach's is always the most extreme, a lot of foleys accompanying the throwing and catching of a pair of underwear, and socioeconomic as they live in a bathroom. A predecessor, without the foleys, is the pool scene of *Tim and Eric's Billion Dollar Movie* (2012) where they are beyond broke, owing a billion dollars, with distinct hairstyles, and Zach (Jim Joe Kelly) makes a lot of Curly/Shemp noises. Zach faints into the pool and Tim and Eric, with physical humor, get him out and begin CPR but they fear he's drying out and push him back in (stooge logic). John C. Reilly is in the film and takes up the third stooge position with the exit of Zach giving a classic Shemp shiver noise during his character premiere.

In the film John C. is also half of a comedy team with Will Ferrell, as the characters Taquito and Uncle Damien Weebs. They provide a few of the highlight reel scenes, though, possibly as a reflection of their relationship, they are rarely together in the same frame. They are an established duo with *Talladega Nights: The Ballad of Ricky Bobby* (2006), *Step Brothers* (2008), and *Holmes and Watson* (2018). So the recipe for *Tim and Eric's Billion Dollar Movie* (2012) was to showcase, arguably, the top two comedy teams in the US.

Character stream is seen in "Tim and Eric Awesome Show, Great Job!: Stuntmen," 2010. The two guest stars, Will Ferrell and John C. Reilly, had recently costarred in *Step Brothers* (2008). Here Tim and Eric play the Stunt Brothers, and also drag parts Lonnie and Marsh. A key plot point in *Step Brothers* was when elementary school bullies beat them up and made them lick white dog sh*t. In "Stuntmen" Dr. Steve Brule (John C.) states, " . . . but what if I could float right over the heads of all the bullies, say nyah nyah [he laughs] how come I can't have that?" For the finale of *Step Brothers*, he did just that, landing in a crowded elementary schoolyard in a helicopter where the two adults proceed to get revenge on the bully children. Also in "Stuntmen" Will Ferrell beats up several of his child clowns and threatens to bury them in the backyard, just like he did to Reilly in *Step Brothers*.[1] Another branch of this character stream leads to "The Oblongs," Will Ferrell played the Dad, Bob Oblong, and as you can see in Angus' *How I Draw* in Color Art, he has no arms. Right after Eric introduces Will as his Dad he picks up a clown and says, "Look at this clown he's got no arms." Further, the creator Angus Oblong makes regular public appearances in clown make up.[2]

---

[1] Ferrell is well known for his odd interactions with children, for example, see either *The Landlord* (2007) where a yelling, beer drinking, and cursing toddler brings him to tears or "Billy On The Street: Scream For An American Girl Doll," 2012 where Will has a screaming contest with three little girls.

[2] Funny or Die, Will Ferrell and Adam McKay's website/production company was involved with *Tim and Eric's Billion Dollar Movie* (2012). Tim and Eric's production company Abso Lutely has further teamed up with the former in "Jon Benjamin Has A Van." Tim and Eric also guest star as aliens in "JBHAV: Star Door" and to further pollute this character stream mix, the prologue to "TAEASGJ!: Stuntmen" has Tim and Eric as aliens.

Orson Welles was an American filmmaker that spent a bit of his career in Ireland and England. Welles at 6'1" teamed up with Russian actor Akim Tamiroff 5'5" to do four films. Their contrasting physiques are a historic ingredient for comedy teams, from Laurel and Hardy, Abbott and Costello, Penn and Teller, Cheech and Chong, to Tim 5'10" and Eric 6'6".[3]

Tim and Eric are a classic comedy team, not only in name, but they are usually together for business: college work; three TV shows and one feature film; comedy tours including them as bandmates; and for interviews and talk shows. They are a good measuring stick to decide just how much of a comedy team a pair of comics are.

There are fewer female comedy teams. Lucille Ball and Vivian Vance worked as a team on three TV shows over 17 years, 1951-68, "I Love Lucy," "The Lucy-Desi Comedy Hour," and "The Lucy Show," but they did not normally appear together for interviews and talk shows. There were two more comedy teams in "I Love Lucy" with pairings of Lucy and Desi, and Fred and Ethel, too. There is "Laverne and Shirley," 1976-83, but due to a disagreement Cindy Williams (Shirley) does not appear in the last 20 episodes. The "Absolutely Fabulous" pair from England, Jennifer Saunders (Edina) and Joanna Lumley (Patsy), have worked as a team on and off since '92, but Saunders also pairs up with cocreator Dawn French. This would be similar to Gregg Turkington now working with only Tim in "On Cinema" and "Decker," while Tim and Eric are still doing "Bedtime Stories."

Dean Martin and Jerry Lewis appeared together in radio, television, audio recordings, live performances, and 16 films, but they did not part amicably. "TAEASGJ!: Anniversary," 2007, from season one, is a parody of this scenario; set in the future, an aged Tim and Eric reunite after a long and bitter separation.

As I was leaving to go and see Tim at his Republican National Convention broadcast, I saw a live TV news clip of an old lady getting jostled around and some arrests, it was getting rowdy on the streets of downtown Cleveland. So, even though I made a Decker For President shirt for the event, I'm wearing it now, I chickened out. A fatal flaw for a comic, never seen with Eric Andre, Derrick Beckles, Sacha Baron Cohen, The Dudesons, John C. Reilly, or Tim and Eric.[4]

---

[3] *Stan and Ollie* just premiered at BFI London Film Festival, John C. Reilly plays Oliver Hardy.

[4] Sacha Baron Cohen, a pioneer in this area, has bodyguards that both protect him and get him to an exit if police inquiry or arrest is imminent per *Independent: Sacha Baron Cohen claims FBI went after him while filming Borat*, Jack Shepard, 2/25/16. Sacha has both American and outsourced Indian teams of lawyers that protect him in his comedy work per *Above The Law: Sacha Baron Cohen Uses Outsourcing For The Win*, Elie Mystal, 4/22/09. Sacha also had one of the best publicists ever in Matt Labov.

"Check it Out! with Dr. Steve Brule," 2010-16.

Creators John C. Reilly, and Tim and Eric.

This show wound up with only 24 episodes; four seasons of six per, every other year. It had the perfect recipe for success: a top name comic actor, John C. Reilly, teamed with now veteran comic directors Tim and Eric (along with Jonathan Krisel); and the three have worked together at Channel 5 News for years-Dr. Steve Brule's show airs at 4:30 AM and he then regularly visits with Jan and Wayne Skylar on their 6 AM "The Married News." The only plausible reason why this show was cancelled? John is so in demand in the film industry that he doesn't have time for a (lower budget) TV show.

Costume is an easily overlooked item in comedy. Dr. Steve wears the exact same mundane outfit for every episode of the series: a dark green suit with an American flag lapel pin, grey shirt, burgundy tie with gold flecks, and brown shoes; he has balding, teased-up curly brown hair, with oval shaped gold metal glasses; and no regular props per se except his lapel or handheld microphone, or set items like his interview chair or glass block half wall.[43] He is a classic intelligence-challenged character, Ali G is an English example. His terrible speech pattern is probably connected to his mental deficiencies, he constantly mixes up nouns, many times adding an "R," pizza to prizza, and has no short term memory for proper names. For the latter in "Health" he interviews an official expert from the U.S. Department of Beauty, Cynthia Driscoll (Maria Bamford), her name is subtitled on the screen and it is likely in his cue cards as well. But he still calls her Samphia Dringus, Cynthia Dangus, Samphia Daglus, and Cynthia Dingus (this is referred to as the name game).

The Beauty Identifier x01.3 is a great prop that tests to see if you are ugly or beautiful (physical characteristics humor). It is an old style computer that has a wide brimmed ladies Easter hat on it along with fake pink roses, lace, and bows. Several pink drapery cords with adhesive ends come out of it and are placed on the patient's face. Dr. Steve registers ugly and Cynthia, in a white lab coat, performs the following full makeover: his hair style now has an extreme flattened part contrasted to his teased up hair; his glasses are removed to show both his partly crossed eyes, and the thick new makeup of blush, green eye shadow, eyebrows, and lip gloss; and he has an added set of of upper prosthetic teeth that are crooked in his mouth. Maria states that out

---

[1] His hair is in the tradition of Larry Fine, Harpo Marx, and Bozo the Clown. The latter was based in Reilly's hometown of Chicago.

of a ten scale he has gone from a one to a three, and Dr. Steve adds, "If three is the best."

In "Friendship" John C. Reilly gets to do a classic drunk character. This is usually accompanied by a disjointed or slurred speech pattern, but Dr. Steve already has this. His new friend takes him to a motorcycle club where he drinks a lot of rye whiskey, some directly from the bottle with the pourer still attached. He stumbles into the bathroom where he vomits three times, then has to go at both ends (also seen in "Planes") so he sits on the toilet, and with audio effects does a double (Hei)decker, and he vomits again after he gets off. At the light of day he awakes in the bathroom and licks vomit from the outside of his mouth and goes on his way. As gross-out humor experts, directors Tim and Eric specialize in feces, while John C. specializes in vomit as seen in "Boats" and more, What are the various recipes for the faux feces and vomit? John C. Reilly is also in *Drunk History Volume 6* on Funny or Die but he's not the drunk character.

A few iconic moments in the history of drunk characters would include Lucille Ball in "I Love Lucy: Lucy Does a TV Commercial," 1952. She is rehearsing a TV commercial for the health tonic Vitameatavegamin, that, unbeknownst to her is 23% alcohol. In a little over eight minutes, she has seven tablespoons of it, then misses the spoon and swigs it out of the bottle, then another spoonful and sops some up with her finger. The strong flavor causes her to shudder for each of the first three tastes, making great faces, here with raised eyebrows and pursed lips, a Lucille Ball trademark now carried on by the likes of Jim Carrey.[2] She has speech problems also, for example, "In this little bottle" becomes "In this biddle lottle." The product name comes out a host of ways including, "Mitameatamigamin," "Mitavatameatyman," and "Vitavatavigivad." After a nap she attempts to sing a Spanish language duet with Ricky on TV.

Richard Pryor also has a few drunk characters. One was from "The Richard Pryor Special," 1977 as Willie, a sad but funny character. The skit goes for ten minutes straight, the length of most Adult Swim episodes, and his costars are John Belushi, the bartender, and Maya Angelou, the wife. In his *Here and Now* (1983) filmed live performance at the Saenger Theatre in New Orleans, he does several drunk characters. Like Dr. Steve Brule, one gets sick and has to, " . . . crawl to the toilet bowl, my place of rest." Richard then makes several great vomit noises as he "decorates" his bathroom.

Richard does an impression of an animal reaction shot in one of the skits, "You wake up in your garage, under your car, dogs be looking at you and sh*t that's when you know you're f##*ed up, when your dog won't come to you!"

---

[2] Jim Carrey is also a great impressionist, see his 1/8/11 SNL skit as a psychic medium.

Pryor has four more animal scenes in this 90 minute comedy performance. In one, an audience member brings him a small live crab in a clear plastic drinking cup. Richard ad-libs the crab's voice, "Why are you f##$ing with me? I was in the ocean, I was just crawling along and some ass##$$ grabbed me." Against the wishes of some audience members, Richard states, "I'm going to take this mother f##$er to the bay or something, put him back in . . . he's gonna live, we gonna save this one . . . cause this mother f##$er did a show."[3]

John C. Reilly also recognizes animal welfare while at work. During a Danish film shoot *Manderlay* (2004), a donkey was slaughtered solely for the purpose of getting the image on film. John C. was the star of the film and walked off the set, quitting the production in protest.[4] This started an even bigger protest against the film, and after replacing John, the director still had to cut all of the donkey scenes from the film before its release.

On occasion John C. plays two characters within the same episode: in "Family" it's Dr. Steve and his imaginary brother Stan. On the evening following his bender in "Friendship," he listens to a street musician in a black fedora, black trench coat, and dark sunglasses, with an alto sax, that he refers to as "the trumpet man." The film that most popularized the dual or multiple character comic role was *The Nutty Professor* (1963) Jerry Lewis, and the subsequent two remakes by Eddie Murphy in 1996 and 2000. Following Jerry Lewis was Richard Pryor in *Which Way is Up?* (1977) where he plays three characters (an image of the trio is in Color Art).

Voice actors for animation normally do dual or multiple characters, for example, Dave Willis plays both Meatwad and Carl on "Aqua Teen Hunger Force," Regina King plays both Huey and Riley on "The Boondocks," and Seth MacFarlane does the majority of the cast on "Family Guy."

Some hunk, a term Dr. Steve Brule uses for men that he doesn't like, must have taken over at Channel 5 as "The Married News" and "Check It Out! with Dr. Steve Brule" have been cancelled!

[3] A stand up comic must be adept at handling hecklers, see Richard Pryor. Hecklers were even present at a charitable fundraiser performance by Dave Chappelle on 7/22/11.

[4] msnbc.msn.com 4/29/04; ew.com 4/30/04; and bbc.co.uk 3/3/05 to name a few. Other classic drunk characters would include Foster Brooks, whose entire comedy career, 1960s-80s, was based on a single character of this type. Sacha Baron Cohen added another layer by playing off of real people, not actors, with real alcohol. In "Da Ali G Show: Respek," 2004 Borat goes to a wine tasting where he drinks nine glasses in a very short period of time; visibly he is at least tipsy, but he is able to stay in character (NOT recommended).

"Delocated," 2009-13.
"Neon Joe, Werewolf Hunter," 2015 to present.
Creator Jon Glaser.

This show is, in part, another "Home Movies" thread. Costar Eugene Mirman still plays a Russian character, but now live-action, Yvgeny Mirminsky. As there are other Russian characters, too, they sometimes converse in their native language and require subtitles. Jon Glaser does comedy performances with Eugene as well as H. Jon Benjamin. H. Jon came up with the idea for "Delocated: Dog Mayer," 2010, and Glaser is in the premiere episode of "Jon Benjamin Has A Van: Borders," 2011. He plays a war veteran who lost his voice thinking about being in the war. So, he speaks in a strained whisper. This is a character stream from his electronically altered voice in "Delocated."

"Delocated" is based on costume, Jon wears a black ski mask at all times. "Tap" contains one of the best comic costumes ever. Jon dons the following: a blue and white trucker hat with the words "FOR LON" (atop his black ski mask); one white sleeveless tee and two tank tops (blue and gray); three polyester running shorts (yellow, red, and orange); a metal urn of his dead parents' ashes placed in a frontpack baby carrier with a customized adjustable plastic rain jacket to cover the top of the urn (details); and a pair of black patent leather tap shoes with black socks. He does a tapathon from NYC to Maine. The bumps stated that the shot of him tapping across the bridge was the first ever helicopter shot for Adult Swim. At the grave he mixes together two famous sayings, and replaces the final word, "Well, I guess the apple doesn't fall far from the chip off the old d*ck."

Amy Schumer played Trish for eight episodes of "Delocated." Jon went on to act in *Trainwreck* (2015) and write for and act in "Inside Amy Schumer."

The subsequent costume based Neon Joe establishes Jon as the leader in this field: light brown regulation haircut with close trimmed beard; neon green attire from head to toe including a sleeveless vest; werewolf claw scars across the left side of his forehead with a black eyepatch; multiple hilarious tattoos such as his "back" story; a functional silver bullet earring; and a silver revolver with bayonet. Steve Cirbus stayed on from "Delocated" and he added a great new comic sidekick, Steve Little as Cleve, who was formally Kenny Powers' (Danny McBride) sidekick Stevie in "Eastbound and Down."[1] He-Yump!

[1] Will Ferrell appears for five memorable episodes of "Eastbound and Down" as supervillain Ashley Schaeffer.

"Eagleheart," 2011-14.
Creators Michael Koman and Andrew Weinberg.

I can't even begin this article in a normal way, the 1961 song "Alley Cat" by Bent Fabric must be playing; give it a listen. This is the lead actor Chris Elliott's trademark, a comic dance to the instrumental version of the song. Coincidently, a 50th anniversary "The Best of Alley Cat" CD was released three weeks after the premiere of "Eagleheart."

Conan O'Brien's company Conaco produces the show, so it makes perfect sense that two of his long time writers from "Late Night with Conan O'Brien," are the creators. Further this is the same genre where Elliott made his mark in "Late Night with David Letterman," 1982-93. He was a writer and did character skits on the show, officially from 1982-88 but the appearances, short films, and skits continued into "Late Show with David Letterman," 1993 to 2015.

There is a lot of precedent for his new U.S. Marshal character in "Late Night with David Letterman," 1982-93. An early skit has him as a member of a neighborhood police watch giving [bad] advice on how to protect yourself on the street. Another running character was *The Fugitive Guy* where in the title sequence he is in a street karate fight. Yet another, was the crime-fighting *The Regulator Guy*; Letterman states about its premiere episode, "Seems pretty violent compared to your past . . . " and Chris concurs that NBC is giving him flak because it is a four minute show with 176 acts of violence. "Eagleheart: Death Punch," 2011 revolves around a rare martial arts punch that explodes its victim into paint drop particles of flesh and blood.[1] It is used on cocaine trafficker Pike, and later on Grandma. For the latter, Elliott and the bedroom are completely covered in blood, he even has his tongue out "catching snowflakes."

Another common term used to describe Chris Elliott is "idiot." Girls especially like to call him this: the adversarial Sharon, his best friend's wife that he trades quips with in "Get a Life," 1990-92; Trina, his love interest in *Cabin Boy* (1994); and Tiffany from "Eagleheart: Death Punch" who is both an adversary and a love interest.

A more recent short film parody, with an appearance in costume on "Late Show with David Letterman," is *Skink The Bounty Hunter* (2007) with Chris and his assistant Gerard Mulligan wearing tin stars in Hawaii. Brett, the assistant

---

[1] A monk uses "the explosive force" killer punch in "Stan Lee's Superhumans," 8/12/10.

to Chris on "Eagleheart" is a smaller version of Gerard with similar looks and demeanor. In "Eagleheart: The Human Bat" Brett stabs the villain repeatedly in the chest with an FX pencil, harkening back to Elliott doing the same to a giant, but with an FX pen, in the finale of *Cabin Boy*.

Another costar in "Eagleheart" is Chief, who is made up to look and sound like Orson Welles' Texas detective character Hank Quinlan from *Touch of Evil* (1958). Elliott has borrowed from classic films before as *Cabin Boy* (1994) was a direct parody of *Captain Courageous* (1937).[2]

Chris Elliott is one of the more knowledgeable active comics, though, still a generation removed from an icon like Jerry Lewis-who knew every trick in the book. His father, Bob Elliott (1923-2016), of the classic Bob and Ray comedy team, costarred with him in the first season of "Get a Life." Chris and Bob had earlier coauthored the book *Daddy's Boy* (1989). Chris was an SNL cast member in 1994-95 and his daughter Abby followed in 2008 as the first SNL second-generation.

In "Eagleheart: A Mug of Chili and a Bowl of Death," Lulu the chef uses U.S. Marshals as her secret ingredient. This cannibal story line is seen earlier in "Get a Life: Camping 2000," 1991 where Chris and his friend are hallucinating on bad berries and believe they have eaten his father. Character streams like this can go on indefinitely as Chris has a large multiformat, book/film/TV, comic vault to reference that even includes an episode of "Miami Vice," 1987.

---

[2] *On Borrowed Time* (1939) provides a character model, almost 75 years later for, of all shows, "Mr. Pickles," 2013.

Stop-Motion

"Moral Orel," 2005-08.
"Mary Shelley's Frankenhole," 2010-12.
Creator Dino Stamatopoulos.

Davey and Goliath," 1960-75, per its website, was a long running stop-motion TV show, 63 episodes and seven specials, from Clokey Productions of Gumby and Pokey fame. The coproducer of the show was the (Evangelical) Lutheran Church In America whose closing credit logo was a space shot of the earth slowly revolving. "Moral Orel" picks up where it left off, as that shot is its opening title. The ficticious Moralton, Statesota reflects Minneapolis, Minnesota the headquarters of the Lutheran Church. The title music is similar, too, as are its respective cast of characters with Pastor Miller and Reverend Putty, etc.

In "Davey and Goliath: Who Me?," 1960 the mom, Mrs. Hansen, wears an apron and is seen twice in the kitchen doing dishes. The Dad is a stern disciplinarian to Davey and relaxes in an easy chair to read his newspaper. In "Moral Orel: Love," 2006 Mrs. Puppington wears an apron and she washes their dinner, a turkey and a live lobster, in the kitchen sink with dish detergent. The Dad, relaxing in an easy chair, lectures Moral about love. Moral gets a dog, Bartholomew, like Goliath, but it talks less. Shapey adds lighter fluid to the grill creating a fire, and says "friend" mimicking the lines of Frankenstein from *Bride of Frankenstein* (1935). The credits show Moral making stop-motion films, here it's a silent film, with only the visuals of Jesus on guitar, and Bartholomew on keyboards.

Late 50s rockabilly and 60s pop into hard rock, added the classic cast of monsters into a slew of songs, with a few literal "monster hits," like Bobby Pickett's "Me and My Mummy" and "Monster Mash," 1962. The following year musician Frank Zappa teamed up with TV horror host Bob Guy, Jeepers, for two singles. The lyrics of "Letter From Jeepers" revolve around Cucamonga, California regional humor, referencing its "great" weather, and local fish and chips recipe, i.e. silverfish and buffalo chips, "the first one went down easy, but the second one was greasy."[1] The local TV horror host here in Cleveland, Ghoulardi, also used regional humor targeting Parma, Ohio with polka music, clothing-white socks, yard ornaments-pink flamingos, and more.

"Mary Shelley's Frankenhole" mixes the classic cast of monsters with a time machine of historic figures. In "Hunger of the Vampire," 2010 Gandhi, who speaks with an Italian accent, visits Dr. Frankenstein for some medical help. Gandhi works up a thirst, " . . . I wouldn't mind a couple of G and Ts right about now" and heads to the local pub, Ye Torch and Pitchfork. One of the bar patrons is Nosferatu and in keeping with the original 1922 German silent film, he has no spoken dialogue, only decorative black-and-white intertitles. The previous year, in 2009, the 2D "The Drinky Crow Show: Aspire" also used a parody of *Nosferatu* and the voice of the lead character Drinky Crow is none other than Dino. Both episodes, one stop-motion and one 2D, and Hutter in the original film, use alcohol as a prop; for Drinky Crow it's the main character's given name and a part of the title of the show. The type of drink identifies the character's traits: Gandhi with a gin and tonic, and Drinky Crow with several bottles marked XXX (in the very first shot of the episode following the title, we see and hear Drinky and Gabby each guzzling a bottle).

What is Ron Burgundy's drink of choice in the *Anchorman* series? In the non comedy genre, What is James Bond's drink of choice? Substances are a very specific costume prop, and if it's a legal item, alcohol and tobacco for example, a possible main source of revenue for the project and its sponsors. Though, if legal or not, tobacco is harmful, so before or after its TV or web appearance would be a perfect spot for an anti-smoking public service ad, as seen on Adult Swim. You can still purchase Ron Burgundy Great Odin's Raven brand Special Blended Scotch Whiskey, and aside from the drink itself comes offshoot products like Ben and Jerry's Scotchy, Scotch, Scotch ice cream, though no longer available, was the company's second most popular limited batch ice cream ever.

---

[1] *Goin Back Radio Show, KRVM-FM,* Dave Gibson, Halloween, 1988 Eugene, OR. globalia.net/donlope/fz. themonster-mash.com.

"Robot Chicken," 2005 to present.

Creators Seth Green and Matthew Senreich.

"Titan Maximum," 2009. Creators Tom Root and Matthew Senreich.

"SuperMansion," 2015 to present. Creators Zeb Wells and Matthew Senreich.

Twisted Toyfare Theater was the comic panel that sparked "Robot Chicken." It started with the Spider-Man Macarena in the first issue of *Toyfare* magazine in 1996.[1] "Robot Chicken" cocreator, Matthew Senreich, was an editor at *Toyfare*. Tom Root, head writer and producer, also came from *Toyfare* (he provides all of the image captions in Color Art). Seth Green, too, has the perfect qualifications: as an accomplished film actor, Scott Evil in the *Austin Powers* series and James St. James in *Party Monster* (2003); as a TV actor with puppets in "Greg the Bunny," 1997; and as the highly recognized TV voice actor for Chris Griffin in "Family Guy." I asked him about his techniques or tips for the latter and he simply said, ". . . to stay focused." He is absolutely one of the leaders in this field as he does maybe 15 different voices PER EPISODE on "Robot Chicken"! It reminds one of the iconic voice actor Mel Blanc, Bugs Bunny et al., who was known as The Man of a Thousand Voices.

"Robot Chicken" is the longest running stop-motion show on TV, and I believe it's also the longest running show of any type on Adult Swim. Stoopid Buddy Stoodios (SBS) has evolved into the premier stop-motion studio for TV and social media.

Ray Harryhausen was a pioneer in this field and one of his unfinished works was pivotal to its revival. He has a large body of work but I'll examine *Mother Goose Stories* (1946), in particular *Old Mother Hubbard*. Nursery rhymes are a great area for research as there are multiple versions over time. His has Mother Hubbard go on four errands to retrieve items for her dog: first for some bread; then the dog plays dead so she gets him a coffin; then shoes; and finally tripe. All the while the dog is doing bizarre things like smoking a pipe, etc. Longer versions of the story can go up to almost a dozen errands, includ-

[1] "TTT first appeared as a secondary feature in 1996's 'Winter Special Edition' of Toyfare -- the first issue of the magazine published -- when Spider-Man taught readers to do the 'Spider-Macarena.' However, the first full-length strip, 'Super Villain Jeopardy,' appeared in the official #1 issue, which was published in September, 1997." Zach Oat, editor of *Toyfare*. per John Rafacz, Wizard Entertainment, 4/25/05. Signs of "Robot Chicken" are seen and heard in "That '70s Show: 5:15," 2004 where Mitch (Seth Green) repeatedly impersonates a chicken with a lot of clucking.

ing getting beer and wine for the dog. So as warped as the story lines of "Robot Chicken" can get, there is some warped historical precedent in this animation style. The early stop-motion process involved switching out character heads, each with a different expression: one with a look of surprise, one with a look of sadness, etc. The four *Mother Goose Stories* contained no dialogue, only intertitles and background music. A later unfinished work, *The Tortoise and the Hare* (1953), contains dialogue, along with a narrator but no lip synch. Per Ray's official site, the '53 project was completed in 2000-01 by Mark Caballero and Seamus Walsh who go on to assist with early "Robot Chicken" and "Moral Orel."

The titles for "Robot Chicken" relate to historic film and TV with the following references: *Frankenstein* (1931)-the scientist and his tagline "It's Alive," the monster, and the set; and the cartoon "Super Chicken," 1967-with a similar logo, and a lively intro song that includes some clucking and an image of Frankenstein.

"Robot Chicken" has been a great TV success, especially the *Star Wars* specials (see more in "Family Guy"), but will Adult Swim ever come up with the capital for a theatrical release film? Twenty-first century stop motion global film revenue, per Box Office Mojo, begins strong with *Chicken Run* (2000) UK/USA/FR, with a 45 million dollar budget and a 225 million dollar box office; and *Team America* (2004) USA/DE follows with a 32 million dollar budget and a smaller 51 million dollar box office. Laika Studios, located in Portland Oregon, is one of the premier stop-motion film studios (its figurine and set dimensions are generally much larger than those of Stoopid Buddy). Its production budgets are all estimated at 60 million and these are the following returns: *Coraline* (2009) at 125 million, *ParaNorman* (2012) at 107 million, *The Boxtrolls* (2014) at 109 million, and *Kubo and the Two Strings* (2016) a bit smaller at 70 million. The "Robot Chicken" five pound pink gummy bear (once sold at adultswimshop.com) would be a great concession item at theatres.

Chickens have not been a prolific species in 2D animation. Possibly because "chicken" has become part of the human vernacular and is associated with coward. Their limited lead character history includes Foghorn Leghorn and Chicken of "Cow and Chicken." All are males, roosters, including Super Chicken, and stop-motion Robot Chicken. Comedy can be both psychoanalytic, a return to childhood, and sexist. "Robot Chicken" has a girl's doll story line with the addition of a boy's action-figure violence, a classic childhood scenario generally only humorous to the male.

Unlike "Robot Chicken," a regular cast was instituted for its following two stop-motion productions: the single season "Titan Maximum," and "Super

Mansion." "Robot Chicken" has a score of recurring characters but not a regular cast per se. In the 100th episode "Fight Club Paradise," 2012 Robot Chicken escapes but has to fight his way up a staircase against such characters as Gummy Bear, Bitch Puddin', Composite Santa, Unicorn, Humping Robot, Adult Swim executives Keith Crofford and Mike Lazzo, Daniel and Nerd who provide no resistance whatsoever, and more. Gummy Bear is edible, she would agree, What if a "Robot Chicken" skit had all of its characters created out of actual edible materials, similar to cake decorations but with flexibility?

The lead cast of "Titan Maximum" was well balanced with two brothers, one chimp, and two females-Jodi and Sasha. Seth Green did the voice of their evil nemesis, Gibbs, and could have done the two female parts as well as he has a great drag voice; for example, his Jenna Bush from "Robot Chicken" or his imitation of Becky in the parking garage scene of *The Italian Job* (2003) US/FR/UK. Adult Swim premiered five TV pilots from 12/3-5/16. The 2D animation "Hot Streets," coproduced by SBS, was one chosen by a viewer poll at adultswim.com to go into production. Seth does an occasional voice or two on the show such as Ambassador Claktar and a Vek narrator in "Hot Streets: Squid of the Dead," 2018.

The Crackle/Adult Swim "SuperMansion," named after its set, has an even more pluralistic cast adding another religion with Jewbot and a geezer character with Titanium Rex, whose name is a play on "Titan Maximum." RIP Brad. "Blark and Son" is a puppet based SBS social media series, Instagram and other, that is also in the process of expanding its cast. Read more about SBS productions in "Family Guy," "Mongo Wrestling Alliance," and the following chapter. Some behind-the-scenes photos and captions from "Robot Chicken" are in Color Art.

Seth starred in the series premiere of "Bobcat Goldthwait's Misfits & Monsters: Bubba the Bear," 7/11/18. He played an animation voice actor (actor/character conflation as the actor, in real life, and the character, in the script, have the same profession) whose cartoon character came to life, no spoiler here, and it's all "The Twilight Zone."

Live Stream Online Programming

The live stream online programming is available 24/7, but the schedule runs from 2:00 PM to midnight Monday through Thursday. There are a host of one hour shows with call-in, chat, and polls: "Digikiss," "As Seen On Adult Swim," "How To Draw," "Stupid Morning Bullshit," "Assembly Line Yeah!" and more.

On a random Thursday, July 26, 2018, two of the shows opened with a live band. "Fishcenter" had Australian Alex Cameron and his band perform and Alex and the sax player visited on the couch for the entire show, they were playing Terminal West in Atlanta that evening. The "Bloodfeast" episode had a live performance by Atlanta's psychedelic band, Chew, from 10:00 to 11:00 PM, normal music venue time, with call-in and chat, while doing that day's New York Times crossword puzzle! It encapsulated the original Adult Swim feeling of, this is awesome, Where else can you see this?

In between these shows at 8:00 PM was "Development Meeting," a groundbreaking idea in the media industry. Walter and Cam are the regular hosts and they usually have a VIP guest, such as show writers and creators of "Mr Pickles," "Hot Streets," and even Senior Executive Vice President of Adult Swim, Mike Lazzo. Seriously, where can anyone make a first pitch directly to the head of a major TV network? Lazzo will also call-in to the show, that means he's listening to it, and provide music video closers. For aspiring show creators, you can download a PDF with Pitch Guidelines at adultswim.com. On this particular evening Cam was off auditioning for SNL, i.e. Adult Swim and comedy.

On Thursday, 4/12/18, Keith Crofford, Executive Vice President of Adult Swim, celebrated his birthday making his first appearance on "Williams Street Swap Shop," it was an anniversary eve for the show, too, at 499 episodes.

"Williams Stream" can be seen on TV from 4:00 to 4:30 AM early Saturday morning. It consists of two one-hour stream shows, edited down to 15 minutes apiece, that rotate weekly. The slot is too small a sample size for a full analysis but on 7/28/18 we have a "Venture Bros." new season promo right before "As Seen On Adult Swim" where Nick sells "Venture Bros." animation cels. There is a Red Bull ad preceding it with a static shot of cartoon fish crossing the screen, just like the live-action "Fishcenter." Nick's first item for sale is an Adult Swim plate with many show characters on it and he points out a fish, "There's 'Williams Stream' that encompasses all of our shows in one fish." Concluding the half hour is a bump with a still photo of a stream in the woods with the text, Watch Our Streams.

Bumps, Ads, and Promos

In the preceding "Williams Stream" 30 minute TV analysis, there was an ad, a promo, and a bump tie-in. Were there also similar story line elements in both shows? This would be standard procedure for FOX animation, Adult Swim, and other networks. All of the shows premiering that block would have one or two of the same story line elements, for example, a reference to the same celebrity and or an instance with breakfast food items. In "As Seen On Adult Swim" the main illustration in the center of the circular plate was a large ship or yacht. In "Bloodfeast" there were numerous lines of dialogue and visuals referencing the yachts in the marinas by Comic-Con. It could be completely random yet it needs to be noted just in case as these were both one hour shows edited down. Analyzing a lengthier section, a two to four hour block, would make it clearer: "Was there an ad that features a boat (such as the *Adrift* DVD release)?", "Did a preceding or following show include a ship (such as "Family Guy: Veteran Guy" where the entire episode revolves around watercraft, from an embroidered ship on a cap to Coast Guard cruisers)?", "Was there a bump that referenced yachts and did it use any relevant background music (such as a clip of "I'm On A Boat" by The Lonely Island featuring T-Pain)?"

Another short example from a different night, 1/23/18, placed a three shot bump before "Hot Streets: The Egg": the first shot was the standard Adult Swim white text on a black background that states, "The following time lapse probably symbolizes something"; the second shot, a time lapse of a bouquet of flowers blooming and then dying; and the third shot, the Adult Swim logo.[1] The line of dialogue, "Stop and smell the flowers," with a few variations, is repeated multiple times and is the theme of "The Egg." In 11 minutes there are seven different sets that contain flowers: a vase in the office; a black-and-white montage placing them in a cave, the mountains, and underwater; a hospital room; a sunflower field; and on a bench. What appears to be a random bump, often is not. A deodorant ad preceded the flower bump with one person giving another a wide berth and the narrator saying, "...smells worse!" In "The Egg" Barry Webbers employs gross out humor and cursing with the line, "I smell like sh#@," and thirty seconds later both French and Branski separately repeat, "Barry smells like sh#@." So there is both a bump and ad tie-in for this episode.

---

[1] Per a music ID app, the background song for the flower bump, "Oirectine" by Boards of Canada, does not appear to tie-in, especially as it is an instrumental with no lyrics.

"Hot Streets: The Egg" both opened and closed with Branski singing "O Sole Mio," indigenous music layered with ethnic/national humor. Music has historically been a large attraction for a young TV audience (see "The Brak Show"). The animated "Freaknik: The Musical" premiered on 3/7/2010 (more on this show in the following article) and I'll list a few promo and ad highlights of this lengthier 60 minute slot. There is a "Superjail!" Season One DVD promo intercut with an added animated character that looks to be bass player/singer Bootsy Collins, with boots, top hat, and star sunglasses.[1] The song he's singing includes the term "Superjail" in its lyrics but it does not register in music ID apps; it's reminiscent of "Wars of Armageddon" by one of his bands, Funkadelic. The music stars of the show, the Sweet Tea Mob, end up in a rough neighborhood of New Orleans and someone puts a gun to Virgil's head. It goes into a freeze frame and a narrator takes over cutting to a single one minute commercial for a live-action film that features guns in a rough neighborhood (edited to mesh with the dialogue, background music, and visuals of the "Freaknik" scene).

In the next commercial break there is a promo for "King of The Hill" with Bobby and Peggy imitating rappers. Following this is a live-action phone ad with brothers parachuting out of a small plane. One minute after this break, in "Freaknik," the Sweet Tea Mob parachutes out of a small plane! Oh, and The Mother Ship lands with an alien Funkadelic to end the musical. There are numerous other tie-in bumps, ads, and promos for this special, too. This was nine years ago and I could go back much further or tune into Adult Swim tonight to see the same model. A prominent business publication contacted me about Adult Swim and it was most interested in this.

---

[1] If memory serves me, there were, earlier in the evening, ads for Bootsy Collins' line of footwear being sold at a national retailer.

Research and Theory

Cartoonography

Cartoons and cartography, I was on a bathroom break at lunch from a Humanities conference, when I returned to the table my spouse and old professor said "Cartoonography" that's a paper we'd like from you. My two favorite people came up with the idea, so no modifications, just do it. There was absolutely no research, that I could find, on this subject, excluding fantasy map analysis. But that's the fun of teaching, and being a student in, a world's only college course like Adult Swim, you can be the first one to research and write about a certain topic. A key element of new topic research is to have a solid foundation with accurate information.[1] This entails working extensively with the original material and not relying on any secondary source information as it is often incorrect. I apply comedy terminology and film methodology to examine cartography in the following three cartoons: a classic Saturday-morning TV series, "The World of Commander McBragg," 1964-66; a postwar short film, *My Bunny Lies Over the Sea* (1948); and a modern TV movie, "Freaknik: The Musical," 3/7/2010.

Commander McBragg is the animation icon of cartography. Though, his character is never shown illustrating a map or globe in the series, he is an enthusiastic and imaginative recipient of these props, whose life revolves around them. The title shot for "The World of Commander McBragg," 1964-66, USA, has its text placed over a spinning globe.[2] The prologue and epilogue for the 48 episodes is usually a three shot comprised of McBragg, a floor globe (sometimes replaced with a travel poster, art object, or map within a book), and an unwitting male acquaintance. In the prologue McBragg points to a spot on the floor globe and it transitions to a planimetric, topographic, or pictorial map of the area. McBragg, as the name implies, then tells tall tales of the region's history with himself as the hero.

Commander McBragg was fashioned after English Hollywood film star Sir C. Aubrey Smith, 1863-1948.[3] Actor/Character conflation folds his English police

---

[1] I have two other world's only college courses in Adam Sandler and Will Ferrell, though they are not as labor intensive as a TV network with online programming.

[2] Like most American animation, part of it was done internationally, here Total TeleVision Productions used both Los Angeles and Mexico City studios. Heintjes, Tom. "Whatever Happened to Total TeleVision Productions?" *Hogan's Alley.* 20 Feb. 2013. Interview with one of the production studio's founders, Buck Biggers.

[3] The format for "The World of Commander McBragg" comes from another Englishman; the live-action "Alfred Hitchcock Presents," 1955-62, USA, has Hitchcock as a television host with props doing a prologue and epilogue. C. Aubrey Smith usually speaks to one or more characters as in "The World Of Commander McBragg," whereas Hitchcock uses a monologue.

and military background into several of his films' story lines. *Unconquered* (1947) USA opens with a classic live-action film cartographic sequence, a narrator retelling history, here English, American, and Native American, over various landscape shots that shift into a map, and in this case the map burns up by means of a flaming arrow.

Several episodes of "The World of Commander McBragg" have an additional title sequence that shows the English Commander leading the US Marines into battle and the subsequent victory celebration. This World War II alliance between the United States and the United Kingdom is seen earlier in the Bugs Bunny 7.5 minute film, *My Bunny Lies Over the Sea* (1948) USA.

Multiple forms of mapping are displayed in this Scottish national comedy short, especially in the titles. Shot 1 is the blue eight ring Warner Bros. logo that mirrors Nicole Oresme's 1377 illustration of Aristotle's (384-322 BC) geo-centric map of the cosmos-eight blue rings with Earth, and the WB shield, at the center, a celestial promotional company map.[4] The eight rings of Aristotle's celestial map relate to the music octave, a much analyzed topic among Greek and later astronomers.[5] The earlier Egyptians used a seven string lyre as an octave, based on their known seven planets; the Greeks then discovered an eighth planet and the music octave has stayed relatively similar since.[6] The WB logo is also seen as a sound/music emblem-a view down the blue eight ringed cone of a megaphone with the WB shield at its mouthpiece, heralding its then new sound film technology "Copyright...The Vitaphone Corp...." The next shot is the Merrie Melodies logo and as a music named company both of the M letters are calligrams of music notes comprised of two upright single flag eighth notes, with the second flag rotated backward.

The WB logo further serves as an introduction to the story line, a blue tunnel or rabbit hole across the Atlantic.[7] The Merrie Melodies logo is next

---

[4] Menut, Albert D, translator. *Le Livre du ciel et du monde.* Edited by Albert D. Menut and Alexander J. Denomy, U Wisconsin P, Madison, Milwaukee, and London, 1968. Nicole Oresme translated Aristotle's *De caelo et mundo,* 350 BC from Latin to French adding commentary and illustrations, some of the latter are not included in this translation. This illustration is from Nicole Oresme's *Le Livre du ciel et du monde,* 1370-77, Paris, BnF, Manuscripts, Fr. 565, fo 69, expositions.bnf.fr.

[5] Director Jean Renoir also plays Octave in *Rules of the Game* (1938) FR, the first letter of the character's name, O, is a circle and would tie-in here with Aristotle's eight ring concentric circle map. The entire film, from the first shot, deals with sound synchronization. Tom Conley has a great discussion on the two balustrade stone globes, terrestial and celestial spheres, in the film, see "Jean Renoir: Cartographies in Deep Focus: Globes In and Out of Perspective" in *Cartographic Cinema,* 2007, pp.59-64.

[6] Chappell, William. *The History of Music. (Art and Science) Vol. I. From The Earliest Records to the Fall of the Roman Empire.* Chappell & Co. and Simpkin & Marshall, London, 1874, pp. lxxix (scale), xliii-iv, 52, 76-86, play.google.com. The aforementioned is an eclectic Victorian work on the ties of astronomy and music, with ancient, Greek, and later octave research. The following are Kepler music and elliptical related: Kozhamthadam, S. J. *The Discovery of Kepler's Laws: The Interaction of Science, Philosophy, and Religion.* U Notre Dame P, Notre Dame, 1994, pp. 22, 35, 74-80, 199, 210. Kepler, Johannes. *Harmonice mundi.* 1619. E. J. Aiton, A. M. Duncan, and J. V. Field, translators. *The Harmony of the World.* Memoirs of the American Philosophical Society, Vol. 209, Philadelphia, 1997.

[7] The WB logo in the closing credits of *My Bunny Lies Over the Sea* is a cropped close-up with a different color scheme and adds the tagline across the center, "That's All Folks!" accompanied by the famous instrumental of the same name.

and features a large blue ribbon medal that takes up more than one-third of its frame. This would serve a mental mapping function as the Blue Riband of the Atlantic, 1840-1973, was an annual prize for the fastest transatlantic passenger liner both eastbound and westbound between the USA and the UK. It was at its height of popularity, breaking the four day barrier with lavish ships, just before a war stoppage in 1939.[8] Some of the liners then provided troop transport and the Blue Riband was on hiatus until 1952.[9] All Blue Riband information was common knowledge to the audience of the original 1948 theatrical release; the blue ribbon of the Merrie Melodies logo signaled its fast and luxurious trip across the Atlantic to the UK (though currently not in service but hopeful of its return) and or veteran war memories.

Shot 3 begins the gender mapping of the opening sequence and shows Bugs reclining atop the letters of his name with mouth wide open inserting a large phallic carrot. This shot could be considered national humor, and may provoke a great reaction shot, as Scotland did not decriminalize private adult homosexual acts until 1980![10]

Shots 4, 5, and 6, the title and credits, are set on a yellow, black, and red tartan background, though of Scottish origin, it is likely not an official tartan pattern but a made up [American] design.[11] Filling in the existing line pattern to create a grid would work out to 11 horizontal lines, making 10 rows, and 16 vertical lines, making 15 columns, to adapt to the 3:2 classic film aspect ratio.[12] The open spaces across the center of the tartan pattern creates one long window with panes, a sill, and partially opened sheer curtains.[13] The sea view through the window shows a calligram of the title as waves (water features are often italicized on maps so this would be a natural progression), and with a lap dissolve Bugs' body subsumes the word BUNNY and he literally lies over THE SEA (the following not in wave calligram and missing Bugs):

MY BUNNY LIES

OVER THE SEA

The art theory behind this title still frame is quite advanced, and would not normally be associated with the genre of cartoons.

Shot 5 continues the nautical theme using tildes, wave shaped dashes, to connect the animation crew to their jobs titles. Shot 6 has an overlay of text,

---

[8] Hughes, Tom. *The Blue Riband of the Atlantic*. Charles Scribbner's Sons, NY, 1973, pp. 9, 165-69.

[9] There are three shots in Alfred Hitchcock's *Saboteur* (1942) that feature two time Blue Riband winner, 1935 and 37, the Normandie. See Francois Truffaut *Hitchcock*, 1967, p. 106.

[10] Johnson, Paul. *Going to Strasbourg: An Oral History of Sexual Orientation Discrimination and the European Convention on Human Rights*. Oxford U P, Oxford, 2016, p. 28.

[11] Trivett, Alan. House of Tartans, Ltd., Perthshire, Scotland, "Help identifying a tartan pattern." Received by author, 22-24 May 2017.

[12] Conley, Tom. "The Letter and the Grid: Geoffroy Tory." *The Self-Made Map*. U Minnesota P, Minneapolis & London, 1996, pp. 62-87.

[13] Hitchcock's *Rope,* released the same year as *My Bunny Lies Over The Sea,* features a large window for almost the entire film with a cityscape instead of seascape, and the later *Rear Window* (1954) has a window title shot, too.

Charles M. Jones (aka Chuck Jones) on the tartan. Neither the iconic director nor the story writer, Michael Maltese, are of Scottish descent.[14]

The title sequence fades to black and the film opens with an aerial tracking shot on a simple topographic map of the UK, the word Scotland zooms in and fills the frame. This aerial view of the UK would be fresh in the minds of the American public, especially veterans stationed there. Scotland was a major air theater, from the first days in 1939 to the very last Luftwaffe air attack of World War II on April 21, 1945.[15]

Bugs makes his character premiere, popping out of a tunnel, the WB logo, with an open map in hand, it is his primary prop for the film. After retracing his route on the sixfold rectangular planimetric map, he mistakes a bagpiper, Angus McCrory, wearing a tartan kilt and tam o'shanter cap (bonnet or bonnie relating to the title, Bunny) for an elderly woman being attacked by a monster. The American rabbit comes to the rescue destroying the bagpipe in implied line cartoon slapstick. Seven comedy terms (national humor, sexual humor-gender identity, physical space humor-being too close to someone, reaction shots, foleys, a costume change, and a composite name tagline) are layered into the following 50 seconds:

Bugs "He put up a terrific battle ma'am, but clean living prevailed...." Bugs pokes him twice in the chest while they lean into each other's personal space. "[H]ay, wait a minute you're no woman, you're a man."

Angus "Certain I'm a man, and what's wrong with that?"

Bugs "What's wrong?" Into a close-up with a nod and a wink to the camera. "What's wrong he says. Why you can't go around like that, it's indecent." Pointing to his tartan kilt.

Angus "Indecent?"

Bugs After a stage left exit and return with two different swoosh foleys, he places a wooden barrel with suspenders over Angus. "It ain't got no two pair a pants but it'll due till you get home." Bugs takes out his map, this time to get directions from Angus. "Now one good turn deserves another, could you point out to me the shortest route to the La Brea Tar Pits in Los Angeles?" [Los Angeles is the location of the Warner Bros. studio.]

Angus "La Brea Tar Pits?" in reaction shot. A crescendo of percussion in the scene's instrumental background music and a stage right exit and return with a rifle, accompanied by two different swoosh foleys. "There are no La Brea Tar Pits in Scotland."

Bugs "Scotland!" in reaction shot, "Mnyeah, what's up McDoc?"

[14] Patrick, Robert. Chuck Jones Center For Creativity, Costa Mesa, California, "Mabel McQuiddy question." Per Linda Jones for Charles M. Jones, received by author, 10 July 2017. The preceding correspondence corrected inaccurate secondary source information that even had an endnote. University of Wyoming American Heritage Center. "Michael Maltese Papers." Biography, Rocky Mountain Online Archive.

[15] Taylor, Les. *Luftwaffe Over Scotland*. Whittles Publishing, Dunbeath, Caithness, Scotland, 2010, pp. 503-4.

Both McDoc and (Commander) McBragg are composite names with the same national, UK, prefix similar to Sigmund Freud's analysis of the occupational prefix in Sensalinger.[16] Angus and Bugs, the only two characters in the film, are a classic comedy team with contrasting physical characteristics and a bit of slapstick. It would be a longstanding character type for at least one of the pair to be in drag. With gender roles being in flux during the war, it was a timely topic. According to Carol Harris, "Trousers were also worn by [UK] women for all but the most formal occasions" (89).[17] As the UK was heavily bombed, there were far more positions for homeland women than in the US. Symptomatic of cartoons, the main cast for the three works examined here, covering a 62 year time period, are all male.

The film title, *My Bunny Lies Over the Sea*, is a play on a version of the second line of lyrics from the traditional Scottish song, "My Bonnie Lies Over the Ocean." Warner Bros. probably could not use the actual song title as it was repopularized in America; a cover single by the Brown Dots was released the same year as the film.[18] This song follows the WB theme, "The Merry-Go-Round Broke Down," as the second instrumental background arrangement of the titles. A "Loch Lomond" arrangement accompanies the establishing shots, beginning with the aerial map and ending on a signpost with a Loch Lomond, a lake in Scotland, directional marker at the top. The marker is drawn to resemble a hand with a pointing finger, a precursor to The Flying Glove and its defeat by the letters of The Beatles' song title "All You Need is Love" in *Yellow Submarine* (1968) USA/UK. The hand marker on the signpost is aligned with the title lap dissolve of Bug's hand on the carrot. "Loch Lomond" was an American hit, too, beginning with Maxine Sullivan's single in 1937, and later released by several artists including Benny Goodman.[19] Sound is a newer addition to the cartographer's toolbox, with the dialogue of Commander McBragg, the narration in Sir C. Aubrey Smith's *Unconquered*, the instrumental theme and background music here in *My Bunny Lies Over the Sea,* or all of the aforementioned plus indigenous music in "Freaknik: The Musical," 3/7/2010.

"Freaknik: The Musical" was a one hour animated film special on the Adult Swim TV network. Freaknic, later Freaknik, was an annual college spring break celebration in Atlanta that peaked in the 90s. "Freaknik: The Musical" likely holds the record for the largest group of popular musical artists in an

[16] Freud, Sigmund. *The Joke and its Relation to the Unconscious.* 1905. Translated by Joyce Crick, Penguin, London, 2003, pp 96-104.

[17] Harris, Carol. *Women At War 1939-1945: The Home Front.* Sutton Publishing, Thrupp, Stroud, and Gloucestershire, 2000. Dobson, Charlotte. The American illustrations of Rosie the Riveter were known to UK women, and one Susan Jones adopted the moniker, "Rosie the Riveter Who Helped Build Lancaster Bombers and Featured in Ewan McGregor Documentary Has Died." *Manchester Evening News,* 7 Feb. 2017.

[18] Warner, Jay. *American Singing Groups.* Hal Leonard Corp., Milwaukee, 2006, p. 16.

[19] Tackley, Catherine. *Benny Goodman's Famous 1938 Jazz Concert.* Oxford U P, NY, 2012, pp. 75-9.

animated work: Snoop Dogg, Lil Wayne, Rick Ross, Kelis, Young Cash, CeeLo Green, T-Pain, and more.

The story follows a young rap group, the Sweet Tea Mob (STM), on their automobile trip with road atlas to the Battle of the Trillest music competition in Atlanta (the location of the Adult Swim network).[20] Several pictorial maps with background music are inserted to trace their impaired and severely meandering southern driving route. These maps are somewhat promotional company, too, as some of the Adult Swim TV shows are both created by artists from the region, set in the region, and occasionally animated there, such as the following: "Squidbillies" cocreated by Dave Willis of, and set in, north Georgia, and animated by Radical Axis of Atlanta; "That Crook'd 'Sip" starring music artist David Banner of Mississipi, and set in Mississipi; etc.[21]

The Boule's six villainous members, parodies of African-American celebrities such as Bill Cosby, do not like Freaknik, and plan out their attacks seated around a giant elliptical world table map.

A burning map is not an uncommon shot in live-action, the title sequences of C. Aubrey Smith's *Unconquered* (1947) or for TV "Bonanza," 1959-73. "Freaknik: The Musical" is a modern cartoon rated TV MA, mature audience only. The following is a 17 second clip of a conversation among STM band-mates traveling in an automobile on the freeway. The MA rating is clear in its two featured comedy terms: substances-alcohol and such are common props and create the classic drunk or impaired character; and cursing-comics can be identified by the number and choice of their curse words, and if they're used within adult material or not.

Virgil "[N]ow where the map at? You smoking the map?"

Doela Man "My bad Virg, I thought that was Zig-Zags [brand of rolling papers]." With a laugh.

Virgil "Now how the hell we supposed to get to Freaknik if you done smoked up the damn map?" [The last three letters of Atlanta, nta, are visible on the burning road atlas joint.]

Doela Man "Man, we don't need no map, you know what I'm saying, with this right here, puff, I'm one with the road." Rear ends the car in front of him, crash sounds.

Anonymous Motorist "What the F*## man, are you blind?"

Doela Man "No, I'm just driving with my eyes closed, sorry." Another crash sound.

---

[20] Akerman, James. "Road Mapping on the Margins." *Library of Congress: Geography and Map Division: From Terra to Terrabytes: The History of 20th-Century Cartography and Beyond, Symposium, Morning Session,* 15 May 2014, (1:50-2:29).

[21] "Freaknik" recycles the following from "That Crook'd 'Sipp," 5/13/2007: the name Sweet Tea; the opening house party set; a geezer wheelchair character; a cameo of Bobo; Caledonia is now named Susie; the van; and the use of pictorial maps.

The first crash shot depicts the road atlas joint as the aftermath of an exploding cigar, an updated spin on this traditional joke shop prop. Coincidently, the same prop can be seen 42 years earlier in another iconic animated musical *Yellow Submarine* (1968) USA/UK, where The Beatles use it on the Boxing monster.[22]

The film ends with narration over an outer space view of Earth. It then shifts from an eye of a dog shaped spaceship to an extreme close-up of Freaknik's mouth. The first credit shot illustrates human sound production through irregular ellipses that are either Freaknik's lips, in an animation of the center of the word elLIPSes, or cartilage and vocal epiglottis rapidly radiating out of frame to "Ghetto Commandments." These closing and credit shots from 2010 recall traits of Bugs Bunny's 1948 WB title logo; the eight ring (octave) promotional celestial map along with the sound production apparatuses of the cone rings and mouthpiece in the megaphone.

The viewer/listener may see and hear a variety of maps that are usually promotional company throughout a film (here animated comedy) but in particular in the title/credit logos and the connecting first establishing and final closing shots. Ending on a "high note," the T-Pain (featuring Snoop Dogg) song continues over the pantomime epilogue showing Doela Man now trying to use cellophane tape (Scotch brand debuted a yellow, black, and red tartan pattern dispenser in 1945 the same era as *My Bunny Lies Over the Sea*) in place of a map, to roll his joint.[23]

---

[22] *Yellow Submarine* (1968) USA/UK celebrated its 50th anniversary with a rerelease into USA/UK theatres in July, 2018.
[23] American Chemical Society. "National Historic Chemical Landmarks: Scotch Transparent Tape." 19 Sept. 2007, asc.org."High note" per Freud *The Joke and its Relation to the Unconscious,* p. 130, "*C)* True double meaning, or *play on words,* the ideal case of multiple use...."

Cartoonography Bibliography

Akerman, James. "Road Mapping on the Margins." *Library of Congress: Geography and Map Division: From Terra to Terrabytes: The History of 20th-Century Cartography and Beyond, Symposium, Morning Session,* 15 May 2014, (1:50-2:29).

American Chemical Society. "National Historic Chemical Landmarks: Scotch Transparent Tape." 19 Sept. 2007, asc.org.

Aristotle. *Aristotle: Complete Works (Golden Deer Classics).* Edhill, E. M., et al., translators, Oregan, New York, 2017.

Bruno, Giuliana. *Atlas of Emotion: Journeys in Art, Architecture, and Film.* Verso, NY and London, 2002.

Chappell, William. *The History of Music. (Art and Science) Vol. I. From The Earliest Records to the Fall of the Roman Empire.* Chappell & Co. and Simpkin & Marshall, London, 1874, play.google.com.

Casey, Edward S. *Representing Place: Landscape Painting & Maps.* U Minnesota P, Minneapolis, 2002.

"Commander McBragg." Golden Cartoons, 2009. The DVD has only 40 of the 48 episodes, the remaining 8 are below. Watched reruns of the series as a youth. For this paper rewatched all 48 episodes twice.

- - -. 22 Nov. 2011, "The World of Commander McBragg - The Himalayas." YouTube, uploaded by bullwinklecanada.

- - -. 15 Dec. 2011, "The World of Commander McBragg - Tightrope." YouTube, uploaded by bullwinklecanada.

- - -. 18 Feb. 2012, "The World of Commander McBragg - The Eclipse." YouTube, uploaded by bullwinklecanada.

- - -. 26 Feb. 2012, "The World of Commander McBragg - Dam Break." YouTube, uploaded by bullwinklecanada.

- - -. 4 May 2012, "The World of Commander McBragg - The Rhino Charge & Around the World." YouTube, uploaded by bullwinklecanada.

- - -. 24 May 2016, "Underdog-The Bubbleheads Parts 3 & 4 - 1964: The World of Commander McBragg: The Giant Elephant." YouTube, uploaded ThreeStrikesOut.

- - -. 30 March 2017, "Commander McBragg 48 The Orient Express." YouTube, uploaded by Ricky Xiong.

Conley, Tom. *The Self-Made Map: Cartographic Writing in Early Modern France.* U Minnesota P, Minneapolis, 1996.

- - -. 2007. *Cartographic Cinema.* U Minnesota P, Minneapolis.

- - -. 2007. "Early Modern Literature and Cartography: An Overview." *The History of Cartography, Volume 3: Cartography in the European Renaissance, Part I.* ed. David Woodward, U Chicago P, Chicago and London, pp. 401-410.

- - -. 2014. "A Haptic Eye." *Society for the Humanities and College of Arts & Sciences Sesquicentennial Conference at Cornell University: Screen Cultures panel of Sensational Humanities,* 1 November. Vimeo, uploaded by Society for the Humanities.

Dobson, Charlotte. "Rosie the Riveter Who Helped Build Lancaster Bombers and Featured in Ewan McGregor Documentary Has Died." *Manchester Evening News,* 7 Feb. 2017.

"Freaknik: The Musical." Warner Bros., Cartoon Network, Adult Swim, 2010. Have seen the film 15 plus times. Here, scanned multiple times, and rewatched the credits and map scenes about 65 times in aggregate.

Freud, Sigmund. *The Joke and its Relation to the Unconscious.* 1905. Translated by Joyce Crick, Penguin, London, 2003.

- - -. "Humour." *The Penguin Freud Reader.* Adam Phillips, sel., Shaun Whiteside, trans., Penguin, London, 2006, pp. 1753-70. 'Der Humor' first published 1927 in Almanach 1928.

Harris, Carol. *Women At War 1939-1945: The Home Front.* Sutton Publishing, Thrupp, Stroud, and Gloucestershire, 2000.

Heintjes, Tom. "Whatever Happened to Total TeleVision Productions?" *Hogan's Alley.* 20 Feb. 2013. Interview B. Biggers.

Hitchcock, Alfred. *Saboteur.* Universal, 1942/2000.

- - -. *Rope.* Universal, 1948/2006.

- - -. *Rear Window.* Universal, 1954/2001.

- - -. "Alfred Hitchcock Presents." Shamley/Universal, 1955-62.

Hughes, Tom. *The Blue Riband of the Atlantic.* Charles Scribbner's Sons, NY, 1973.

Jameson, Fredric. *Cognitive Mapping.* 1990. Eds. C. Nelson and L. Grossberg. *Marxism and the Interpretation of Culture.* U Illinois P, (S. 347-60; m. Diskussion), http://www.rainer-rilling.de/gs-villa07-Dateien/JamesonF86a_CognitiveMapping.pdf, ND.

Johnson, Paul. *Going to Strasbourg: An Oral History of Sexual Orientation Discrimination and the European Convention on Human Rights*. Oxford U P, Oxford, 2016.

Kepler, Johannes. *Harmonice mundi*. 1619. E. J. Aiton, A. M. Duncan, and J. V. Field, translators. *The Harmony of the World*. Memoirs of the American Philosophical Society, Vol. 209, Philadelphia, 1997.

Kozhamthadam, S. J. *The Discovery of Kepler's Laws: The Interaction of Science, Philosophy, and Religion*. U Notre Dame P, Notre Dame, 1994.

Looney Tunes Golden Collection: My Bunny Lies Over the Sea. Warner Bros., Disc 1 track 11, ND. Watched the entire film 20 plus times, and rewatched the titles and map scenes well over 100 times aggregate.

Metz, Christian. *Psychoanalysis and Cinema: The Imaginary Signifier*. Britan, Celia, Williams, Annwyl, Brewster, Ben, and Alfred Guzzetti, translators. Macmillan P, London, 1983, academia.edu.

Muehrcke, Phillip C. and Juliana O. *Map Use: Reading, Analysis, and Interpretation*. JP Publications, Madison, 1978.

Oresme, Nicole. *Le Livre du ciel et du monde*. Eds. Albert D. Menut and Alexander J. Denomy, trans. Menut, U Wisconsin P, Madison, Milwaukee, and London, 1968. Oresme translated Aristotle's *De caelo et mundo*, 350 BC from Latin to French adding commentary and illustrations, some of the latter are not included in the Menut translation. The illustration is from Nicole Oresme's *Le Livre du ciel et du monde*, 1370-77, Paris, BnF, Manuscripts, Fr. 565, fo 69, expositions.bnf.fr.

Patrick, Robert. Chuck Jones Center For Creativity, Costa Mesa, California, "Mabel McQuiddy question." Per Linda Jones for Charles M. Jones, received by author, 10 July 2017.

Renoir, Jean. *Rules of the Game*. France. Janus, Criterion, 1939/2011.

Short, John Rennie. *The World Through Maps: A History of Cartography*. Firefly Books, Toronto, 2003.

Tackley, Catherine. *Benny Goodman's Famous 1938 Jazz Concert*. Oxford U P, NY, 2012.

Taylor, Les. *Luftwaffe Over Scotland*. Whittles Publishing, Dunbeath, Caithness, Scotland, 2010.

Truffaut, Francois. *Hitchcock*, Touchstone, Simon and Schuster, New York, 1967.

Trivett, Alan. House of Tartans, Ltd., Perthshire, Scotland, "Help identifying a tartan pattern." Received by author, 22-24 May 2017.

Unconquered--gary cooper 1947. YouTube, uploaded by Robert Harrison, 3 June 2015.

University of Wyoming American Heritage Center. "Michael Maltese Papers." Biography, Rocky Mountain Online Archive.

Warner, Jay. *American Singing Groups*. Hal Leonard Corp., Milwaukee, 2006.

Woodward, David. "Cartography and the Renaissance: Continuity and Change." *The History of Cartography, Volume 3: Cartography in the European Renaissance, Part I*, ed. David Woodward, U Chicago P, Chicago and London, 2007, pp. 3-23.

Yellow Submarine. USA/UK. Music and epilogue The Beatles, Subafilms/MGM, 1968/1999. Have seen the film 15 plus times. Here, scanned twice, and rewatched the Flying Glove and exploding cigar scenes four times each.

Glossaries

Comedy

classic character types new employees, geezers, drunks, gangsters, space aliens, historical figures, etc.

costume is comprised of the following three items (literally getting into character):

A) makeup-including hair color and style, facial hair, and prosthetics.

B) clothes type-details from hat down to footwear.

C) props-such as transportation, substances (alcohol, tobacco, marijuana, and drugs), weapons, musical instruments, and even animals.

gags multiple people simultaneously entering a doorway; a food fight; etc.

gait, posture, and dance details of their style and form, generally including ineptitude, are key traits in creating a comic character.

geezer humor one of the easiest targets for jokes, old folks and their aging issues: deterioration of mental and physical health; lack of independence and finances; keeping up to date with technology and trends; their challenged love life; etc.

gross-out humor puke, poop, farts, snot, odors, belches, etc.

interaction of a duo, trio, or group usually involves contrasting physical characteristics, slapstick, and can include a constant power struggle for who is in charge.

juvenile humor comic basics arise from tactics endemic to children up to eight years old: comic rhymes, making faces, mimicry, etc.

national humor spotlights the stereotypes of a country/nation, usually other than your own. Palestine and Israel for the American viewing audience of Adam Sandler's *You Don't Mess With The Zohan* (2008) USA; Israeli Zohan's obsession with hummus (food) and hacky sack (sports); and Rob Schneider's Palestinian character Salim's mispronunciation of "liquid nitrogen" or Nasi's confusion over soup and soap (accent). If the person is an immigrant it is ethnic/national humor.

parody play on popular films, TV shows, books, or music. To get the most from this type of humor, the audience needs to have familiarity with the original work that the parody is based on. As this is not always the case there must be another level of humor involved.

physical characteristics as with many of these terms it can be used as a cruel form of humor, from common height and weight jokes to the uncommon Oblongs.

physical humor dance, pantomime, pratfall, slapstick, etc. Includes physical space humor such as getting too close to someone.

political humor with a show or episode title "Tom Goes to the Mayor" or "Metalocalypse: Dethgov"; or just a character such as Ronald Reagan in Brad Neely's "China, IL: The Diamond Castle," or his early *George Washington* short.

pratfall falling and landing on your butt.

regional humor spotlights various stereotypes in a specific region of your own country: accent, food, sports, costume, music, holiday/festivals, and geography. Apply the preceding to Boston, Hawaii, New Orleans, etc. You can be of any race, ethnicity, or religion and still exhibit regional stereotypes.

repetition and multiplication repeating dialogue over and over accompanied by multiples of a character or object. Do actual counts.

set up "This is a priceless antique; please take extraordinary care when moving it . . . ."

sexual humor often sexist including anti-gay and pornographic. Purposeful incorrect gender ID. Double entendres.

slapstick rough physical humor, could involve blows, characteristic of most cartoon violence. It can also be used as an expression of endearment. Do a hit count.

snowball effect and amp up Both terms are interchangeable, the former may increase the severity of a disaster, while the latter may increase things in a positive manner. Make a chronological list of steps.

socioeconomic humor traditionally busting on the wealthy but also the poor.

speech

A) vocal volume level-whisper to yell; pronunciation-accent on the wrong syllable; impediments-stutter, stammer, lisp, etc; and noises. Pantomime-the suffix explains this "mime" no vocal-includes physical gestures like yes or no head nods, and mouthing words.

B) tactics foreign/regional accents; made up languages; babble; literal interpretations; malapropisms; impersonations; repeat back incorrectly-the most common form is the name game; reword an old proverb; and cursing-choice and amount of words (never spell them out, even in a quote, replace a letter or two with a symbol).

C) voice actor the age and sex of the actor versus the age and sex of the character. Simultaneous dialogue-two or more characters speaking at once. Multiple voices via multiple characters by a single actor.

stooge logic free association slapstick; uncommon or overly simplistic ways from point A to B. The Stooge recipe-hairstyles, slapstick (foleys should accompany), trio, socioeconomic, and no regular set. Also Speech A) noises as from, real brothers, Curly or Shemp.

Animation

actor/character conflation events from the personal life of an actor or voice actor (not from their earlier acting roles) are partially scripted into the character he or she plays as most of the audience is familiar with this information through celebrity media.

animatic a limited resource layout of a new show or episode. Usually keyframes with audio and a few scenes partially or fully animated.

approaches to animation (most of this is applicable to live-action).

A) character profile age, sex, income, region, etc.; construction and proportions taking note of outstanding or omitted physical characteristics; costumes; shadows and light source; character premiere; usual sets-urban or rural, home or workplace, detail in the backgrounds, anachronistic set; character commercial endorsements; etc.

B) historical research film, comedy, and/or animation timeline with predecessors, concurrent offshoots, and followers (includes relevant world history); era technology; compare and contrast with the pilot, and if it is a remake or recycled the original; prime time cartoon history; origin in print media as a book or newspaper strip? etc.

C) theoretical psychoanalytic, semiotic, or merging disciplines, etc.

D) show breakdown when and where it's made; for what audience; network; time slot; cost; run time; number of episodes; animation method; studio or location; hired laughers or laugh track including its volume and frequency; has it branched out into other media formats; marketing; company, cast and crew affiliations and background, including work relevant biographic information; and ratings or box office numbers (both domestic and international).

E) writing styles are different throughout industry and academia;

TV and popular music titles (AP style) are quotation mark, show title, colon, episode title, comma, quotation mark, followed by the year, "Bob's Burgers: Paraders of the Lost Float," 2017 or use the exact air date 5/21/17. The TV show or episode title by itself is in quotes "Bob's Burgers." If it's a lengthy title "Tim and Eric's Awesome Show, Great Job!" you can shorten it to an acronym or initialism, TAEASGJ! is alone without quotes, but with the episode title "TAEASGJ!: Dads." A song title example is "Yellow Submarine," 1966. There is a film of the same name released two years later but you can recognize the media type by writing style.

Film, artwork, and book titles (almost universal except for AP style) are italicized followed by the year in normal print, in parenthesis, and add country if other than USA: *Yellow Submarine* (1968) USA/UK (so this is a dual country production).

CAA computer assisted animation includes modeling, inbetweeners, mouth movements, backgrounds, fill color, shot types, etc. Computer generated imagery, CG, can save time and money and is more three dimensional.

continuity break an animator or animation company whose work on an episode/series is incongruent, through error, dated information, or constraints of recycling, with that of the whole. An article of clothing, for example, might change from blue to green, and back again, within the same scene. Common in live-action films with reshoots and pick-ups.

illustration checkpoints black-and-white or color, suggested movement, light source and shadows, background detail, number of characters, all three costume items, angle of view, pose, and facial expression.

implied line lines that suggest direction, motion, and contact but in real life either can't be seen or are barely discernable.

inbetweener drawings added to connect or complete the motions in-between the keyframes; see the following.

keyframe drawing of an important frozen moment of an action. Similar to comic book or graphic novel drawings but more frequent.

onion skin a great animation tool that allows you to see your previous drawing(s) underneath your current drawing so you can accurately position set items and better gauge character movements.

phoneme particular sounds or letters of speech. Character mouth movements coincide with them.

recycle to reduce the time and expense of creating new animation, you reuse, for example backgrounds within the same episode or series, or even for other company shows. Williams Street reuses parts of the cels of "The Space Ghost," 1966-68 for "Space Ghost Coast to Coast," 1994-2008.

surreal dreamlike or nightmarish instances that are not physically a part of our normal everyday world, for example being punched by a figure in a painting.

timing the amount of animation per shot length.

traditional animation a minimum of 12 drawings is needed for one second of screen time, or at least 720 per minute. This time consuming process can vary but generally consists of first a hand drawn image which is then hand traced onto a cel, it is then hand painted, and set up to be filmed (little has changed since post WW1).

Film

VISUAL: camera placement point up to a subject is **low angle** (subject is in control) versus point down to a subject or **high angle** for the opposite effect. Camera placed exactly where the eyes of a character are located is a **point-of-view shot**. A tilted or "crooked" camera is **oblique angle**. Camera placed behind a partially opened object of the setting, an ironwork fence, for example, is a **shoot through**. A **track shot** physically moves the camera and its support base, while a **pan** rotates only the camera from a fixed base position. An **over the shoulder shot** usually alternates this camera position between two people in a conversation. **Camera height,** low to or high off of the ground is another element. You can mix and match all of the above.

cause to effect edit first the cause, spoiled food; then cut directly to the effect, events in the bathroom (both can be by visual and/or audio means). You can also place in-between a cutaway shot or scene.

character stream a long standing live-action film technique that occurs scores of times in most films. Character elements, such as dialogue, sets, traits, and costumes, from earlier film/TV/web roles of an actor are fashioned into the scripts of their successive characters, especially if the preceding were successful. It creates a brand identity.

deep focus applies receding focal points (see below) to the frame; fore, mid, and background are simultaneously in focus.

film movements some of the films from the following Western movements include great comedy, and some can be used as origin material for parody: Dada 1917 to mid 1920s; German Expressionism 1919-33; Surrealism 1924 to mid 1930s and beyond; French Realism 1930s; American Film Noir early 1940s to early 1950s; Italian Neorealism 1945-52; and French New Wave 1957-62. Characteristics of the individual movements define the look and feel of your project.

focal point(s) areas within the frame designed to draw your attention. Current style has only one point whereas you may have a more complicated version with from two to several points of comedy, either working in conjunction or competing, in the same frame.

frame divider a visual marker, such as a post, placed between characters that show their current or coming narrative divide.

framing gag crop off part of the frame to hide some action or the punch line. You can then reveal an unexpected person, place, or thing; or just shield the mechanics of a gag, like a clown car.

long shot people are very small in the frame in relation to their surroundings, and this causes ambiguity. Appropriate for a pantomime of idiots loose in a particular environment, or for distance gags. May have a better audience reception in large screen projection.

long take turn on a single camera, begin the shot or take, and let it run -uninterrupted-anywhere from a minute up to the length of the entire scene, show, or film. A realistic type of humor that includes all minutia, every moment of real time.

mise-en-scene an object of the setting (artworks, clothing, jewelry, furnishings, architectural elements, etc.) that provides narrative, autobiographical, historical, or other information. The object in the frame is sometimes supported by dialogue, and is often a premonition of the story line to come.

reaction shot displays the expression of what another person thinks of a character's actions. It is both the intended result of, and usually funnier than, the comic action itself. A person, normally in a one shot, appalled or surprised by certain behavior.

single shot/one shot one person "all alone" in the frame.

transitional devices include a wipe, a lap dissolve, a jump cut, and an iris. How are the various audio tracks treated with it?

two shot two people "together" in the frame. Some comedy teams (duos) stay in two shots for near the entirety of a film. One of the rare separations might evolve from a two shot conversation that escalates into an argument, first a frame divider might appear, then they will be placed at opposite ends of the frame, and finally they will be in single shots (the latter can also be layered with high and low angle to indicate who won the argument).

AUDIO: ambient sound environmental background sound that adds realism, for example, outdoors-a bird chirping, or indoors-the noise produced by an air-conditioner.

background music no visible on screen origination point for music (that is NO musician, electronic device, vinyl turntable, CD player, TV, etc.). Add the following details: the style of music; the song title and year; and the writer, lyricist, and performer.

deep sound deep focus audio. Do the levels correspond with the action and natural relative distances of the fore, mid, and background?

foley a new, more comic, sound is added to replace the natural sound of an action.

indigenous music has a visible on screen origination point.

narration/voice-over is it a character in the film (check the proper spelling of the name and add the actor's name, too), a host, or other?

theme music introduces, a title song, and closes, a credits song, the work. Does it recur within and, if so, where and how many times? Who is the writer and performer?

Color Art

Courtesy of Stoopid Buddy Stoodios

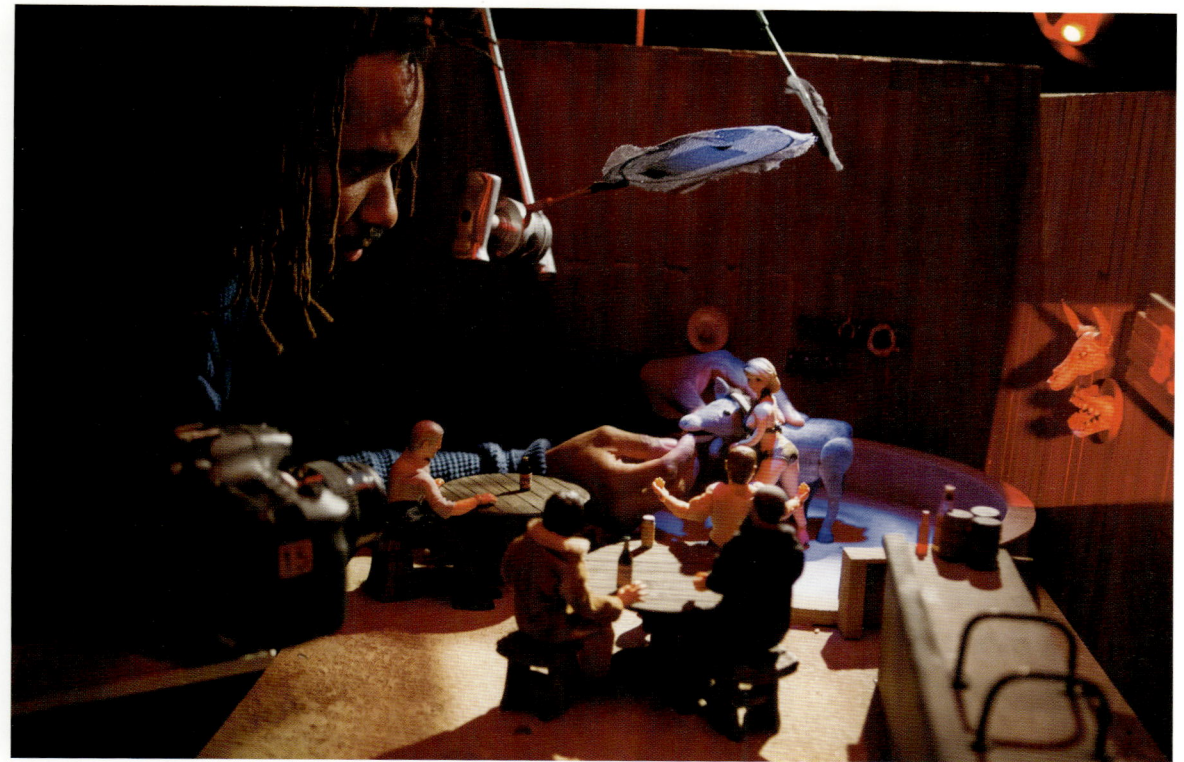

“Animator Brandon Lake makes some final up-close tweaks on a Robot Chicken stage.”

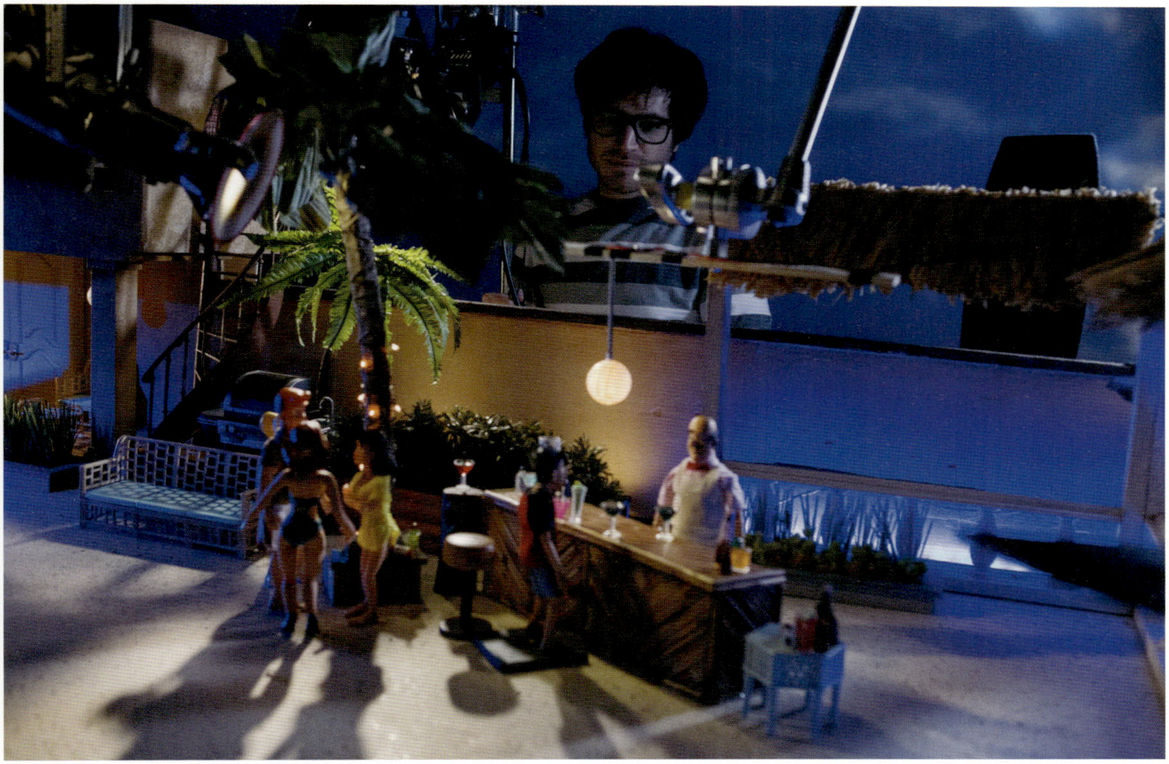

Courtesy of Stoopid Buddy Stoodios

“Camera operator Andy Knapp is the perfect example to show the scale of the Robot Chicken stages.”

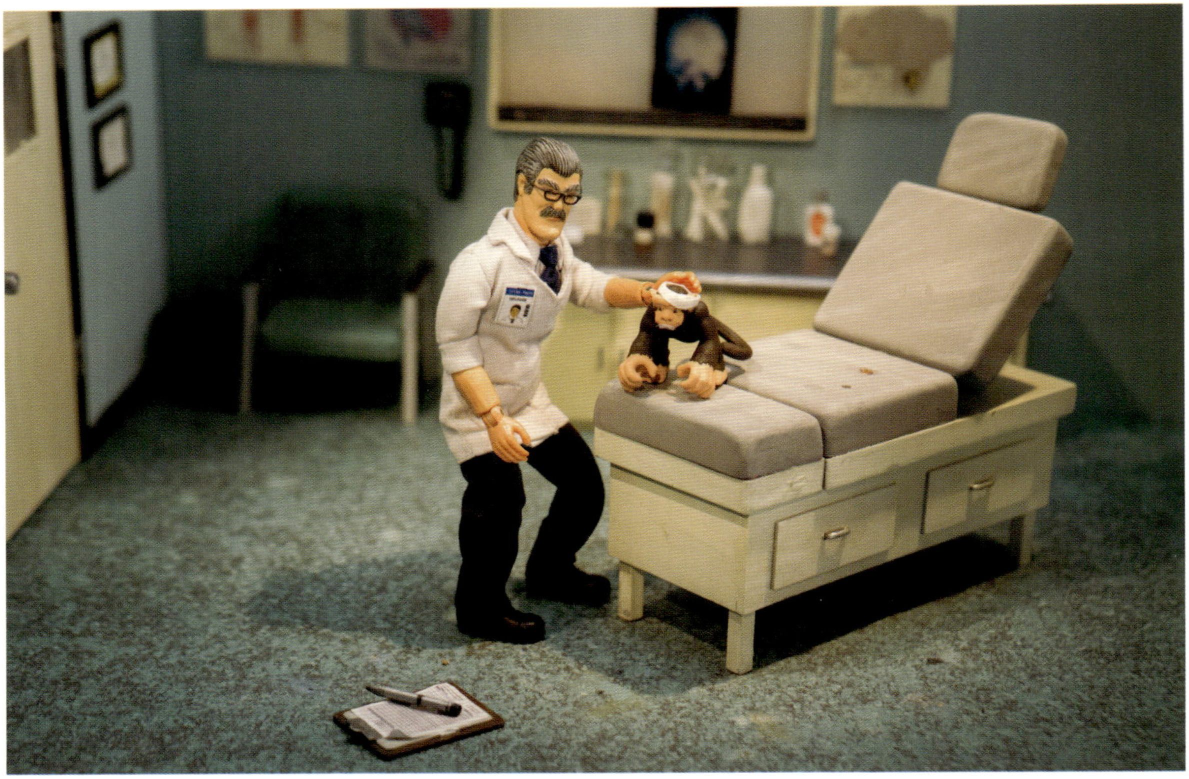

Courtesy of Stoopid Buddy Stoodios

"Only the best puppet veterinarians are brought on to fix up the puppet animals on Robot Chicken!"

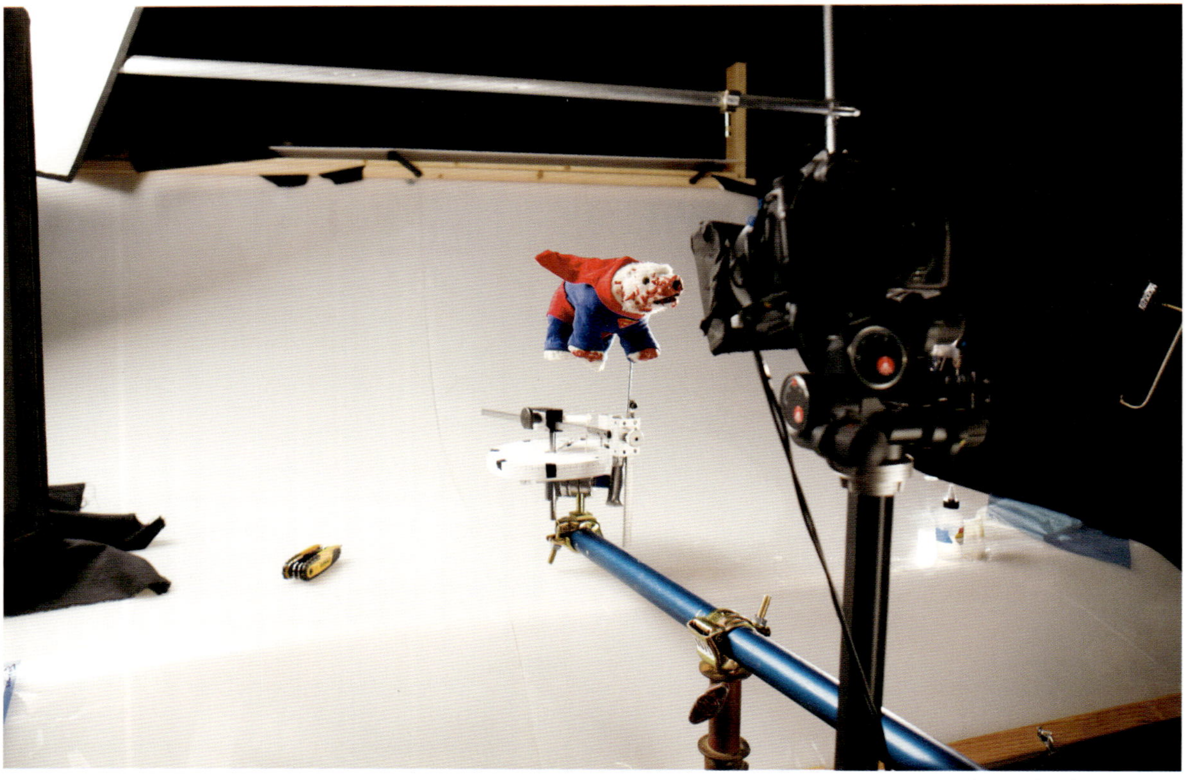

Courtesy of Stoopid Buddy Stoodios

"Rigs are used whenever puppets need to fly or fall. The VFX team edits them out in post."

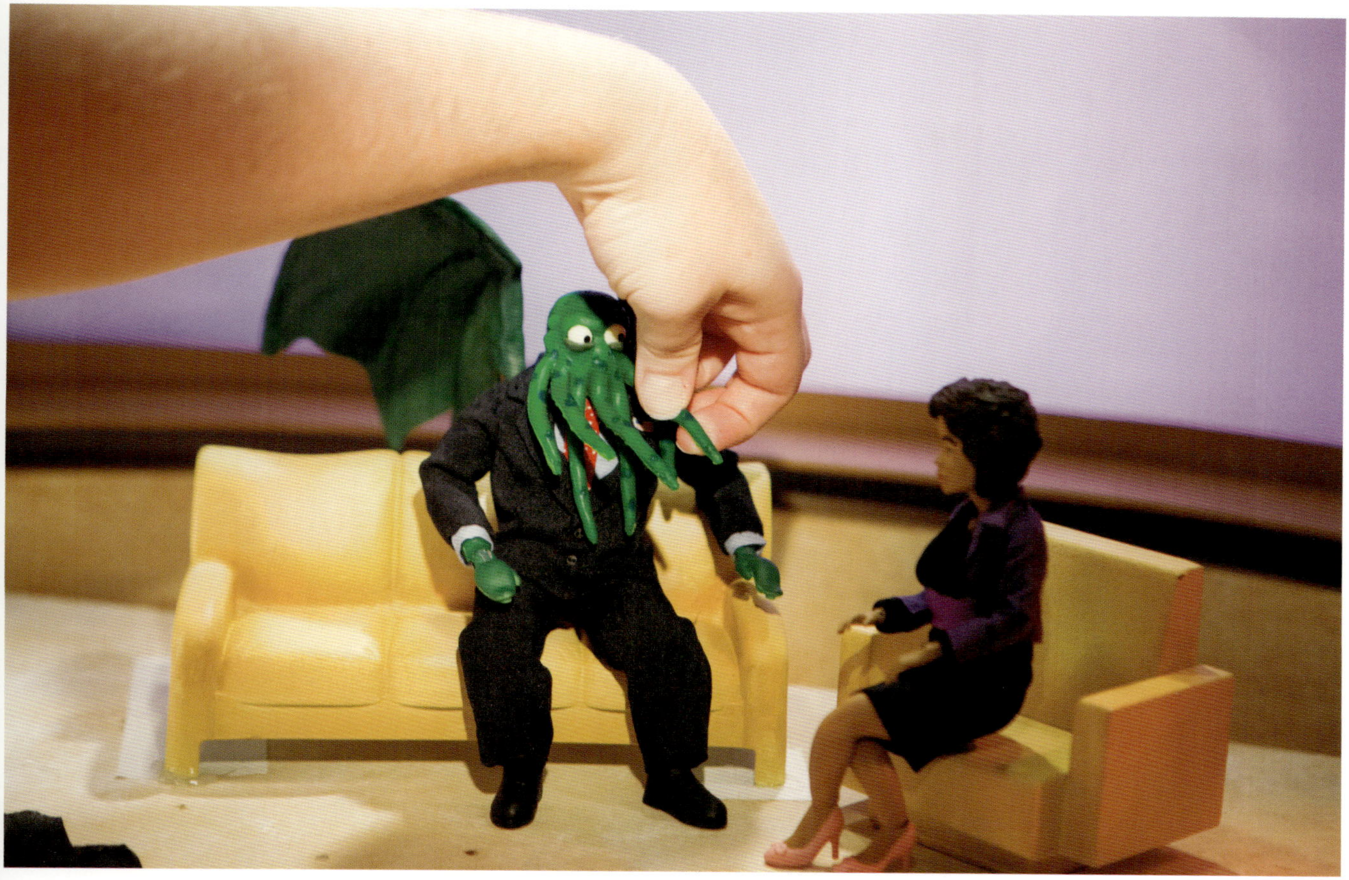

Courtesy of Stoopid Buddy Stoodios

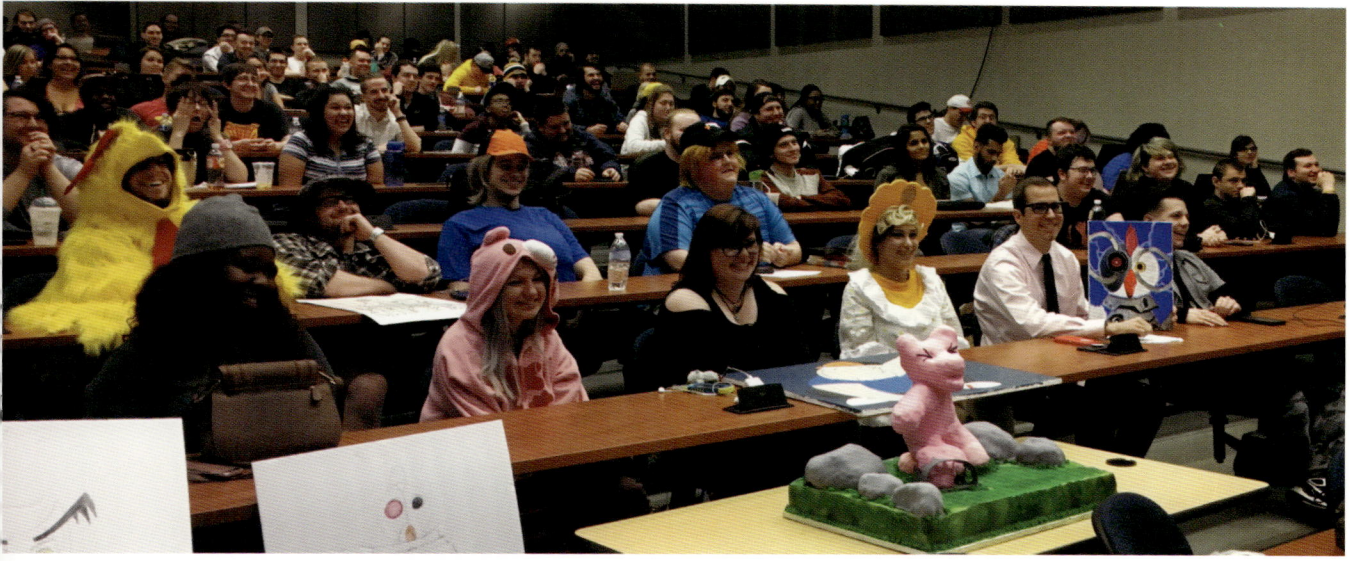

"Even Lovecraftian cosmic entities need a touchup or two on set."

Seth Green teleconference with the Adult Swim class. Costumes include Gummy Bear, and accompanying cake, Bitch Puddin', Nerd, Chris Griffin twins, and many more. Artworks include posters, paintings, and a sculpture. All received extra credit but Seth had to pick a winner-the Chris painting behind the cake. To finish the telecon, the class became an enormous choir clucking the "Robot Chicken" closing credit theme song! We practiced a lot.

Opposite, above, and below:
World of Tomorrow Episode 2: The Burden of Other People's Thoughts C) 2017 Don Hertzfeldt.
All images courtesy of bitterfilms.com.

"Great White North," 1981 hit #1 album in Canada and #8 in USA. Includes the single "Take Off" featuring Geddy Lee of Rush. The McKenzie Bros. are Rick Moranis and Dave Thomas, both images courtesy of the latter. Canadian national humor and costume.

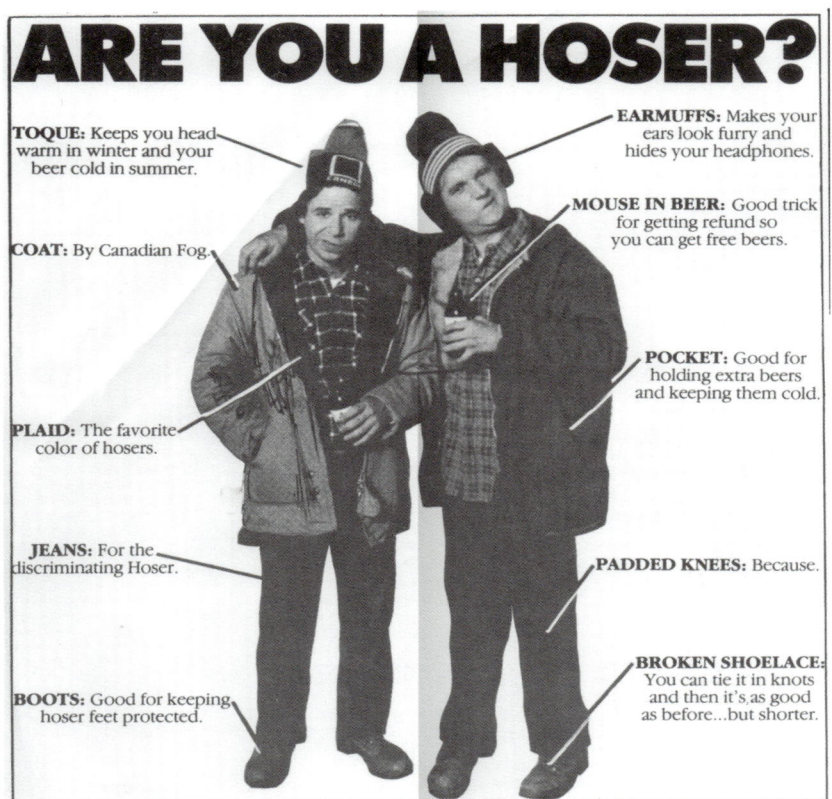

On the set of *My Breakfast with Blassie* (1981). From bottom right counter clockwise: wrestling icon Classy Freddy Blassie, Johnny Legend, Linda Lautrec, and Hollywood star and wrestler Andy Kaufman wearing a neck brace, his signature prop. Courtesy of the directors, Lautrec and Legend.

Before the Adult Swim course was held in an auditorium, a smaller class in a teleconference with Jon Glaser of "Delocated." We had a 9' party sub, a skins bar, and some great artwork. Jon said he would talk to us for as long as we could keep the ski masks on. This was a great lesson in understanding what it's like to work in an extreme costume for any length of time.

No school funds were used for this or Seth's telecon: I purchased the party sub and all of the ski masks for this, and the cake for Seth, and the students provide their own artwork and costumes.

Larry and Steve (1996). Seth MacFarlane's follow-up to his RISD college short film, *The Life of Larry* (1995). The characters are precursors to Peter and Brian in all aspects except their final look and name (common in animation). Both images courtesy of Seth MacFarlane.

Above: *Hunter At Speed* by Ralph Steadman. This illustration and the one opposite top left were on the same page in the last edition. It inspired one of the coolest cutaways ever in "Family Guy: Tea Peter," 5/13/12 with Chris Griffin as Hunter S. Thompson in *Fear and Loathing in Las Vegas: A Savage Journey to the Heart of the American Dream.*

Below: *Study in Gamboge Hat*, 1981, Ralph Steadman. Hunter is the inspiration for Colonel, now General, Hunter Gathers in "The Venture Bros." Both images courtesy of the artist, ralphsteadman.com.

Richard Pryor's comedy lives on as does his animal welfare foundation, Pryor's Planet. He plays three characters in *Which Way Is Up?* (1977): **L to R** Leroy Jones; his Pop, Rufus; and Right Reverend Lenox Thomas, Pastor. Courtesy of Jennifer Lee Pryor.

Tim and Eric's Billion Dollar Movie (2012): **opposite top**-a musical character premiere for Taquito (John C. Reilly); **above**-Tim and Eric with Jim Joe Kelly (Zach Galifianakis); **below**-Tim and Eric with Damien Weebs (Will Ferrell) in a near 7 minute scene, also see the 15 minute version in Extended Scenes. The film is a study in comedy duos and trios. All images courtesy of Abso Lutely Productions.

An illustration of C. Aubrey Smith by cocreator of "The World of Commander McBragg," Chet Stover. This is the English actor the cartoon Commander is based on. Fellow cocreator Buck Biggers provides a great model for Adult Swim personnel as he wrote all of the music and cowrote the scripts with Stover. "Underdog," "Tooter Turtle," and "Klondike Kat" are a few of the other shows by the Total TeleVision team. Courtesy of Victoria Biggers.

CHUCK JONES™ Center for Creativity

Art by Eric Goldberg, courtesy of CJCC with Wile E. Coyote and Roadrunner, Marvin, Bugs Bunny, etc. This great educational facility in Costa Mesa includes a museum, gift shop, events, and lots of animation classes!

Agnes and Her Dead Husband's Ashes. by Angus Oblong.

How I Draw Stuff.

by Angus Oblong.

I start with a light blue pencil, sketching the general shapes of my characters. Then add the black ink, Once the ink is dry, I erase the pencil lines. Then add color. I have tried many different types of pens and colored markers, and prefer (for black) Microns. And for color, Prismacolor markers, because they tend to not bleed or smudge the Microns. Especially on watercolor paper.

Now keep in mind that I'm not encouraging you to illustrate in my style, but to find your own and work with that. I'm simply showing you how I do the crap that I do.

Angus Oblong.

Helga.

Creepy Susie.

Bob Oblong.

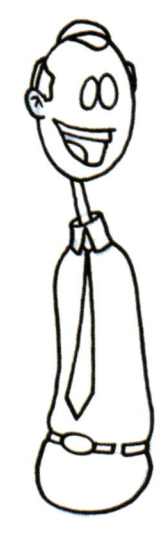

Angus Oblong...

Griffin.